Czech
in Three Months

Elisabeth Billington

A DK Publishing Book

www.dk.com

A DK PUBLISHING BOOK

www.dk.com

First American Edition, 1999
10 9 8 7 6 5 4 3 2 1

Published in the United States by
DK Publishing, Inc.
95 Madison Avenue
New York, New York 10016

Library of Congress Cataloging-in-Publication Data
Billington, Elisabeth.
Czech in three months / Elisabeth Billington. -- 1st American ed.
        p.   cm. -- (Hugo's simplified system)
        "Hugo's language books."
        Includes index.
        ISBN 0–7894–4399–6 (alk. paper). -- ISBN 0–7894–4433–X
        (w/cassette)
        1. Czech language--Textbooks for foreign speakers--
        English. I. Title. II. Title: Czech in 3 months. III. Series.
        PG 4112.B55 1999
        491.8'682421 -- dc21   98–31745
                                                                CIP

Set in 10/12pt Palatino by
Cooling Brown, Hampton, Middx
Printed and bound by LegoPrint, Italy

Contents

3

Preface

This course has been written for those who want to be able to use the Czech language in a more varied range of situations than the stock phrase book scenarios, "At the Airport", "Booking a Hotel Room" and so on: by the time you have worked through the chapters in this book, your understanding of the language should enable you to construct the sentences needed in such circumstances for yourself.

Having said that, we wouldn't want you to imagine that you will be "speaking like a native" in three months, nor is this a course for the aspiring student in Czech linguistics – it does not cover every aspect of Czech grammar, but only those we consider necessary for a solid foundation. Our aim is to provide you with a sound understanding of the basic grammar needed to express yourself in virtually any context on a visit to the Czech Republic. The flexibility you will achieve means that it is immaterial whether you are there on holiday or on business, although the dialogues are set in social, rather than business, contexts. The structure of the course is such that, whatever your own needs in terms of vocabulary, you will be able to use words you find in a dictionary in a way which is grammatically correct.

Our experience of language teaching has shown that one of the difficulties which most frequently blocks students' progress in learning a foreign language (particularly when working without a teacher) is a lack of familiarity with the structures of English, and of grammatical terms in general – the function of an adverb, for example, or what is meant by the "accusative case". We therefore briefly explain such terms when they first occur (if you have studied German or Latin, you may find that you can skip some of this explanatory text). Unless you've an understanding of these matters already, it can be daunting and confusing to discover that Czech has seven "cases" and four "conjugations"; the plethora of word endings that arise from these might appear to owe their existence to perversity – but they don't! Wherever possible, we have tried to explain Czech grammar with reference to English, so that you will understand the construction of the Czech language and hence when to use all these different endings.

There are no complex rules for working through the course which you must memorize beforehand. You are given instructions and suggestions at the point in the chapter where you are required to do something or might welcome some sort of "hint"; where we think it possible that you might have forgotten something, we include either a brief reminder or a cross-reference – sometimes both. All you need do is begin at Chapter 1 and follow our instructions.

Ideally, you should spend about an hour a day on your work, although this is by no means a hard-and-fast rule. Do as much as you feel capable of doing at a particular time; if you don't have a special aptitude for language learning, there's no point in forcing yourself beyond your daily capacity to assimilate new material. It is much better to learn a little at a time, and to learn that thoroughly. At the beginning of each day's session, spend ten minutes recalling what you learned the day before. When you read the Czech words and dialogues, say them out aloud if possible. Study each rule or numbered section carefully and re-read it to ensure that you have fully understood the grammar and examples given. Try to understand rather than memorize; if you have understood, the exercise will ensure that you remember the rules through applying them.

A set of cassette recordings is available with *Czech in Three Months*; although these tapes aren't an integral part of the book course (which is perfectly viable without them), they are bound to help you with your pronunciation. Remember that there are far fewer opportunities for you to hear spoken Czech than (say) French or German, were you to be studying either of the latter languages. The cassettes cover in detail the sounds of Czech, set out in Chapter 1. They let you hear many of the model words and sentences found in subsequent units, as well as all the dialogues which close each chapter.

You'll be able to test your grasp of vocabulary by responding to a verbal "prompt", and some of the written exercises may also be adapted for oral practice.

When the course is completed, you should have a good knowledge of Czech – more than sufficient for general holiday or business use, and enough to act as a basis for further studies. We hope you enjoy *Czech in Three Months*, and wish you success in learning.

Acknowledgements

Very many thanks to Hannah Kodiček for her help in ensuring the idiomatic accuracy of materials in this course, particularly in certain dialogues, and for many other suggestions. Thanks too, to Danny Kodiček for reading through the text and checking details. Their joint injection of enthusiasm and encouragement has been invaluable.

Picture Credits

Jacket: all special photography Clive Streeter and Peter Wilson except IMPACT: Peter Sellers front centre above right; NEIL SETCHFIELD: top left centre, centre below right, bottom centre, back.

Chapter 1

1.1 Pronunciation

In this chapter, you will learn the basic rules of Czech pronunciation. Having said this, we do not expect you to be pronouncing Czech like a native when you have completed it! A written guide to pronunciation, no matter how extensive, can only ever be an approximation – and often the written description will "click" only after actually hearing the words being spoken. You can see, then, that it would be counter-productive to try to memorize everything that is described here. We would recommend that you work through this first chapter, quite slowly and carefully <u>once</u>, and, having done so, move straight on to Chapter 2 and start to get to grips with learning the language. This chapter will always be here for you to come back to whenever you wish, and you will probably find it easier when you are using it in conjunction with words and phrases whose meaning you understand. You could, for example, use a few minutes at the end of each study period to practise saying some of the sentences in the chapter you have been working on with this pronunciation guide in front of you.

If you have the cassettes which accompany this course, then your life becomes a lot easier because you will be able to copy the native speakers on the tape – and you should, of course, take every opportunity to listen to spoken Czech.

Although you may not understand very much of it at first, you will still absorb the rhythms and stresses of the language.

For now, then, work through the paragraphs which follow and pronounce the sounds described <u>out loud</u>. You'll probably feel pretty silly – especially when you are practising single vowel or consonant sounds – but surely this is better than articulating nothing until you are facing an expectant-looking Czech and realize that, although you could write what it is you want to say, you are tongue-tied with embarrassment at the idea of hearing yourself speak Czech! Better to cringe for an hour or so NOW! As you work through the course you will lose your self-consciousness: first, you will become more familiar with hearing the foreign language coming from your own mouth (as will anyone who might be around while you are learning!); second, as you become able to work with the language, building up your own sentences and understanding the meaning of whole strings of words, your pronunciation will naturally acquire the assurance which comes from knowledge that you are making progress.

In the paragraphs which follow, we give English words which have similar sounds in them to the Czech sounds we are describing. Say the English words out loud too; <u>think</u> about the sound you are making in English, so that you can transfer that sound to the Czech word which follows.

The English words printed in *italics* are translations of the Czech examples, given so that the latter have some significance for you. We don't mean you to learn them at this stage. You should be concentrating on learning Czech pronunciation, not vocabulary.

1.2 Stress

The stress is always on the first syllable of a Czech word. If you are not quite sure what this means, then say: "father", "meadow", "gallery", "rocking". The stress in these words is on the first syllable. But in "postpone" and "tomato", the stress is on the second syllable – and in "exhibition", it is on

10

the third. We shall have a little more to say about stress in paragraph 4.9, but this is the basic rule and is sufficient for you to be getting along with until then.

1.3 Vowels

When you are pronouncing the words in this section, don't worry about the consonant sounds. In fact, relatively few of them are different from their English equivalents and you can come back to the words in this list after working through paragraph 1.5. For now, simply concentrate on getting the <u>vowel</u> sounds correct.

Czech and English both have the five vowels: **a e i o** and **u**. In addition, Czech pronounces **y** exactly the same as **i** and so we shall treat the two together here.

a	resembles the unstressed article "a" in English, as in "a crab", or the "u" in "cup", but is clearer, so try the Czech: **maso** (*flesh*); **nalevo** (*left; on the left*)
e	resembles the "e" sound in "set", "get" and "den", but is more open, so try: **den** (*day*); **jeden** (*one*)
i/y	both resemble the "i" sound in "bit" and "sit", but are more closed, so try: **pivo** (*beer*); **miska** (*dish*); **tady** (*here*); **knihy** (*books*)
o	resembles the "o" sound in "not" and "hot", but is more open, so try: **ano** (*yes*); **voda** (*water*)
u	resembles the "u" sound in "book" and "look", but is more tense, so try: **student** (*student*).

In addition to the five plain vowels and "y", Czech can add an acute accent to each of them: **á é í** (and **ý**) **ó** and **ú**. We also have **ů** which is pronounced in exactly the same way as **ú**. When to use **ú** and when to use **ů**? We use **ú** at the beginning of the word, and **ů** in the middle or at the end of it.

This is something you will get used to as you come into contact with written Czech.

The effect of the accent is to lengthen the vowel: you should make accented (long) vowels sound almost twice as long as unaccented (or short) ones. If you're not sure, compare the long and short English sounds in the rough-equivalents (e.g. "seat" and "sit") and then transfer these sounds to the Czech.

á   resembles the "a" sound in "far", "father" and "large": **káva** (*coffee*); **tabák** (*tobacco*)

é   resembles the "e" sound in "bed" and "melt", but is slightly longer: **mléko** (*milk*); **léto** (*summer*)

í/ý   both resemble the "ee" sound in "weed" and the "ea" sound in "seat": **jídlo** (*food; meal*); **prosím** (*please; that's OK*); **sýr** (*cheese*); **východ** (*exit*)

ó   resembles the "aw" sound in "law" and "raw": **vagón** (*wagon; carriage*); **citrón** (*lemon*)

ú/ů   both resemble the "oo" sound in "food" and "stool": **ústřední** (*central*); **úterý** (*Tuesday*); **stůl** (*table; desk*); **průvodčí** (*bus conductor*).

1.4 Diphthongs

A diphthong is where two vowels together make one sound. Two examples in English are "seat" and "mouth" – we don't say "see-at" "moh-uth". Czech has three such combinations: **ou**, **au** and **eu**.

ou   resembles the sound made by "oh" in English: **novou** (*new*); **koupelna** (*bathroom*)

au	resembles the "ow" sound in "cow" or "clown": **auto** (*car*); **automatický** (*automatic*)

eu	resembles the "eu" sound in "Amadeus": **neurologie** (*neurology*).

You will not come across the **eu** diphthong to the same extent as the **ou** or **au** ones. It tends to feature only in words which have been imported into the Czech language from elsewhere.

1.5 Consonants

There are 25 consonants in Czech (see paragraph 1.7), many of which are pronounced as they are in English. In this paragraph, we deal only with those which are different.

c	resembles the "ts" sound in "treats" or "splits": **cizí** (*foreign*); **cukr** (*sugar*); **clo** (*customs; duty*)

č	the accent above the **c** is called a hook or **háček** and the sound of **č** resembles the "ch" sound in "cheese" or "itch": **čáp** (*stork*); **čistý** (*clean*)

ch	resembles the guttural sound in the Scottish "loch" – which, remember, is NOT like "lock"! – so try: **chalupa** (*cottage*); **chytrý** (*clever; intelligent*)

j	resembles the "y" sound in "you" or "yes": **já** (*I*); **vejce** (*egg*); **jíst** (*to eat*)

k	these three sound the same as English but without
p	aspiration (try not to "p-puff" air out at the end):
t	**káva** (*coffee*); **pivo** (*beer*); **teta** (*aunt*)

r	is rolled much more than English ("vrrroom"): **rok** (*year*); **ráno** (*morning*)

ř	has a shorter roll, run together with the "z" sound of "s" in "vision" or "pleasure": **říjen** (*October*); **jiřina** (*dahlia*)

13

š	resembles the "sh" sound in "ship" or "mash": **široký** (*wide*); **šála** (*scarf*)
ž	resembles the "s" sound in "leisure" or "vision": **žába** (*frog*); **žlutý** (*yellow*)
ď ň ť	these three are soft (palatal) when followed by **a, or** or **u**, or when they stand at the end of the word: **teď** (*now*); **žízeň** (*thirst*); **labuť** (*swan*)
ď	in all other circumstances than those described above, resembles the "d" sound in "dew" and "duty" as it slides into the following vowel: **řiďte** (*drive!*); **veďte** (*lead!*) – both commands.
ť	in all other circumstances than those described above, resembles the "t" sound in "tune" and "Tuesday" as it slides into the following "u": **síť** (*net*)
ň	in all other circumstances than those described above, resembles the first "n" sound in "companion" as it slides into the following "i": **laň** (*doe*)
di ni ti	when followed by "i", as here, these three are pronounced just like the three immediately above: **divák** (*spectator*); **tichý** (*quiet*); **nikdo** (*nobody*)
dě ně tě	these three combinations are also pronounced softly: **děj** (*story; plot*); **někdy** (*sometimes*); **těším se** (*I am looking forward*)
bě pě vě	imagine a Czech **j** between the two letters of each combination (-bjě-; -pjě-; -vjě-) to soften it: **běh** (*to run*); **pěkný** (*nice*); **věnec** (*wreath*)
mě	sounds as if it were written -mně-: **měsíc** (*moon*); **město** (*town*).

At this point, you might like to run through your pronunciation of the words in paragraph 1.3 to confirm that you know what to do with their consonants as well as with their vowels.

1.6 Voiced and voiceless consonants

Read through this paragraph, but don't agonize over it or allow it to bog you down. As you get used to hearing Czech spoken, and to speaking it yourself, the instructions here will probably come naturally, without conscious effort, but we are including them now so that you will understand how spoken Czech relates to what you see on the printed page.

A "voiced" consonant is one which is uttered with resonance of the vocal cords; a "voiceless" consonant is one produced with the breath only. Say aloud the words "big" and "pig", and isolate the sounds these start with, to help understand what we mean. In spoken Czech, many of the voiced consonants have voiceless counterparts which are used only in the middle and end of words. For example, voiced "b" and "d" are replaced respectively by unvoiced "p" and "t" – with the result that what's spelt as **obchod** sounds like *op-khot*. Have a look at the following table:

Voiced	Voiceless	Example	Imitated pronunciation
b	p	**obchod** (business, shop)	*op-khot*
v	f	**dívka** (girl)	*d'yeef-ka*
d	t	**předsálí** (foyer)	*przhet-sah-lee*
d'	t'	**jed'te** (go! i.e. a command)	*yet'ye*
z	s	**hezký** (attractive; pretty)	*hes-kee*
ž	š	**těžký** (difficult; heavy)	*t'yesh-kee*
h	ch	**lehký** (easy; light)	*lekh-kee*

As we said, don't get bogged down with this: it's something that you can expect to acquire gradually over a number of months' contact with the spoken language – not something you can learn from the printed page in half-an-hour. Remember that consonants at the beginnings of words are always pronounced as described in paragraph 1.5 above.

Now try Exercise 1.1. If you have the tape, you will be prompted to speak the first word, after which you will hear it repeated by the native Czech speaker. If your pronunciation is a reasonable match, then you should speak the next word and so on. If what you hear is markedly different from what you said, then stop the tape and have another go. Repeat the exercise until your pronunciation matches that on the tape at least 80% of the time.

Exercise 1.1

Say the following words out loud:

nalevo; káva; jeden; mléko; miska; prosím; východ; ano; průvodčí; cizí; chalupa; jíst; ráno; říjen; široký; žlutý; ted'; žízeň; řid'te; labut'; tichý; těším se; pěkný; měsíc; obchod; dívka; odjezd; jed'te; hezký; těžký; lehký.

Now try some phrases:

Nerozumím.	I don't understand.
Mluvíte anglicky?	Do you speak English?
Mluvte pomalu, prosím.	Please speak more slowly.
Jmenuji se [your name].	My name is …
Těší mě.	Pleased to meet you.
S dovolením.	Excuse me, please.
Promiňte!	Sorry! (an apology)
Můžete mi pomoci?	Can you help me?
Kde je záchod?	Where is the toilet?
Kolik to stojí?	How much is it?
Nevím.	I don't know.
Správně.	That's right.

1.7 Hard and soft consonants

Before embarking on this topic, which is fundamental to Czech grammar, both written and spoken, you should be clear that this has nothing to do with pronunciation: the pronunciation is as we have taught it to you above, and as you heard it on the tape.

The consonants in Czech are divided into three groups – hard, soft, and neutral – as follows.

Hard:	h; ch; k; r; d; t; n; g
Soft:	ž; š; č; ř; ď; ť; ň; c; j
Neutral:	b; f; l; m; p; s; v; z

The consonants "w", "x" and "q" are considered to be foreign to Czech, and you would meet them only in words imported from other languages.

This notion of hard and soft consonants has no equivalent in English. It is one of the most "foreign" aspects of Czech, and something with which you'll have to make a little effort to become familiar. Whole words in Czech can be "hard" or "soft" depending on the characteristic of the final consonant. This, in turn, has implications for the various endings which are taken by the word in question and for other words in the sentence which are related to it. All of this may sound terribly daunting but once we begin to see it working in the language, you'll find that it soon soaks in, so don't worry. You might find it useful at this stage, though, to write the consonant groups (as they are shown above) on a small postcard which you can use as a bookmark. It will then be ready for reference when you need it, without your having to turn back to this page in the book every time you need to know the status of a consonant.

Here are two rules for distinguishing "hard" and "soft" nouns.

1   Basically, it is the <u>final consonant</u> of the noun in the nominative singular case which determines whether that

noun is hard or soft, so you should check the consonant against the list above.

2   If the last letter is **i** or **í**, or **y** or **ý**, you can tell straight away:
    soft = **i** or **í**
    hard = **y** or **ý**.

Here are some examples.

Hard: **most** (bridge); **hlad** (hunger)
Soft: **věc** (thing); **řeč** (language)
Neutral   **pes** (dog); **vůz** (car; wagon)

1.8 The Imitated Pronunciation

Our system whereby the pronunciation of Czech words is imitated by English syllables is maintained throughout Chapters 2–4 and should be seen as a "last resort" aid; far better that you should do as we've just suggested, and refer back to sections 1.2–1.7 as you progress. If you have the audio cassettes, listen to them carefully.

Remember that the imitated pronunciation is only an approximation, and that it is based on standard (British) English sounds. Here is a summary of how we've interpreted some of the special characteristics of Czech – our imitations are shown in italics:

a, e, i/y, o, u [*a, e, i/i, o, u*]: the short vowels; when you see these imitated in *to, do* or *ye*, keep them short – <u>don't</u> say "too", "doo" or "yee". Don't forget that when **e** comes at the end of a word, it must be pronounced as a separate syllable.

á, é, í/ý, ó, ú, ů [*ah, eh, ee/ee, aw, oo, oo*]: the long vowels.

au, ou [*ow, oh*]: note *ow* as in "cow", <u>not</u> "low".

ě [*y'e*]: as *ye* in "yet".

dě, ně, tě [*d'ye, n'ye, t'ye*]: the **ně**, for example, as *ny* in "canyon".

bě, pě, vě [*b'ye, p'ye, t'ye*]: the same as above.

mě [*mn'ye*]: note the insertion of an n-sound.

d', t', ň [*d'y, t'y', n'y*]: when followed by **a, or** or **u,** or at the end of a word, is a soft palatal sound (don't give much value to the *y*). When the letter is in other positions, see below.

d', t', ň, di, ti, ni, dí, tí, ní [*d'yew, t'yew, n'yew*]: like *de/te/ne/* in "dew", "tune" and "new".

c [*ts*]: as *ts* in "cats", "treats".

č [*ch*]: as *ch* in "cheese", "itch".

š [*sh*]: as *sh* in "ship", "mash".

ž [*zh*]: as *s* in "leisure", "vision".

r [*r*]: always remember to rrroll the plain Czech *r* well.

ř [*r'zh*]: a shorter rolled *r* plus *s* as in "vision".

h (at word end), **ch** [*kh*]: a guttural Scots *ch* as in "loch".

j [*y*]: as *y* in "yes", "you".

That completes the first chapter. In those which follow, we shall be laying the foundations of Czech grammar; as you work through them, say the Czech words out loud whenever possible (and always properly to yourself – don't just "think" them). Refer back to Chapter 1 every so often, to make sure that you remember the ground rules.

Chapter 2

- *Greetings*
- *Nouns and personal pronouns in the nominative case*
- *Verbs "to be" (být) "to have" (mít), and reflexive verbs*
- *Adjectives and pronouns in the nominative case*
- *Surnames, nationality and professions*

2.1 Greetings, everyday phrases

Throughout the day, one of the greetings you will hear most often is **Dobrý den** (literally, "Good day"). In English, we tend to respond to greetings such as "Good morning", "Hello", "Good evening" with exactly the same words. Czechs do the same thing, and so the correct response would be **Dobrý den**.

When taking leave of the person, you say **Na shledanou** (or just **nashle** if your relationship with the other person is an informal one). Literally, this expresses the hope that you will see the person again.

In the evening, the most usual greeting is **Dobrý večer** and, again, you would say the same in reply.

There are a couple of greetings which are used in informal situations, such as between friends or members of a family. These are **ahoj** and **nazdar**. Ahoj and nazdar mean both "hello" <u>and</u> "goodbye", and so the same greeting is used on parting as was used when meeting. Neither is preferable to the other, although you will probably find **ahoj** used more frequently, **nazdar** tending to be used by older people.

Here are some more useful phrases for you to use straight away.

Dobré ráno or **dobré jitro**	*Good morning* (in the early morning)
Dobrou noc	*Good night* (when going to bed)
Děkuji	*Thank you*
Děkuji vám	*Thank you* (with special emphasis on "you")
Dík or **díky**	*Thanks*
Není zač	*You're welcome; don't mention it*
Prosím	This word has many meanings, including: *please; here you are; pardon?*; and you will also hear it as a reply to **děkuji** (i.e. when we might say *It's a pleasure*)

IMITATED PRONUNCIATION (2.1): *dob-ree den; nas-khle-da-noh; dob-ree-vetch-er; a-hoy; naz-dar; dob-reh rah-no; dob-reh yit-ro; dob-roh nots; d'yek-oo-yi; d'yek-oo-yi vahm; d'yeek; d'yeek-ki; nen-ee zatch; pros-seem.*

2.2 Nouns: gender

Nouns are the words we use to represent people, things or concepts e.g. Mary, cat, beauty, man, castle, justice.

In English, we classify people into masculine and feminine, while inanimate objects (things) are neuter. In Czech, as in English, human beings and animals are either masculine or feminine according to their actual sex. However, there are two important differences:

(a) nouns denoting children and the young of animals are neuter;
(b) masculine nouns are divided into animate and inanimate.

The nouns which describe things, and which would all be neuter in English, are divided among the different genders in Czech. The ending of a Czech word is a guide to its gender, as shown in the examples on the following page.

Gender	Common ending	Examples
Masculine	Consonant	**pán** (*gentleman*); **muž** (*man*); **student** (*male student*); **stůl** (*table*); **dům** (*house*); **doktor** (*male doctor*); **lékař** (*male physician*); **byt** (*flat* or *apart ment*)
Feminine	Vowel **a**	**žena** (*woman*); **dáma** (*lady*); **studentka** (*female student*); **dívka** (*girl*); **doktorka** (*female doctor*); **lékařka** (*female physician*); **kniha** (*book*)
	Vowel **e**	**židle** (*chair*); **růže** (*rose*); **učebnice** (*textbook*); **tabule** (*blackboard*); **přítelkyně** (*girlfriend*)
	Consonant	**skříň** (*cupboard*); **místnost** (*room*); **věc** (*thing*); **žízeň** (*thirst*)
Neuter	Vowel **o**	**město** (*town*); **okno** (*window*); **kolo** (*bicycle*)
	Vowel **e**	**moře** (*sea*); **kuře** (*chicken*); **děvče** (*girl*)
	Vowel **í**	**náměstí** (*square*); **nádraží** (*station*)

IMITATED PRONUNCIATION (2.2): *pahn; muzh; stu-dent; stool; doom; dok-tor; leh-karzh; bit; zhen-a; dah-ma; stu-dent-ka; d'yeev-ka; dok-tor-ka; leh-kharzh-ka; k'ne-ha; zhid-le; roo-zhe; oo-cheb-n'yits-e; taboo-le; pr'zhee-tel-ki-n'ye; skrzheen'y; meest-nost; v'yets; zhee-zen'y; mn'yes-to; ok-no; ko-lo; mor-zhe; kur-zhe; d'yef-che; nah-mn'yes-t'yee; nah-dra-zhee.*

These are not rules, but more of a rough guide; your best plan is to learn the gender of the noun along with the noun itself.

You may be wondering why this matters. It is important because other parts of speech take different forms according to the gender of the noun with which they are associated. This seems unnecessarily convoluted to English speakers. After all, if we want to describe someone as, say, "good", the word "good" does not change in any way whether it is a man, a girl or a dog who is "good" – we say, "a good man", "a good girl", "a good dog". In Czech, however, as in many other languages, the word describing the noun (the adjective) is formed differently for each gender. If you do not know the correct gender of the noun, therefore, you are likely to make mistakes with the words you want to use in connection with it. (Adjectives are dealt with in paragraph 2.9 below.)

Exercise 2.1

Using the table above to help you, group the following nouns into masculine, femine and neuter. (We have not provided translations of the new words here, since this would give the game away! Apart from **divadlo** *(theatre), however, they are not too dissimilar from their English equivalents.)*

auto	sestra	Petr
matka	parlament	Martina
žízeň	bratr	restaurace
divadlo	kino	
prezident	moře	

2.3 Nouns: case

In English, nouns do not change their form or spelling no matter what part they are playing in the sentence. Look at the following two sentences: "The dog chased the ball." "The girl patted the dog." The word dog plays a different part in each sentence: in the first, it is the dog who is carrying out the action; in the second, the girl is carrying out the action and the dog is having the action carried out on him. In the first example, we say that the dog is the subject of the sentence; in the second, the dog is the object of the sentence. But, in each case, the word "dog" is the same. This is not true of Czech – the noun changes its form according to its role in the sentence, and this is expressed by using different cases. There are seven cases in Czech, and we shall explain each one as we meet it.

2.4 Nouns: nominative case

This is the name given to the form of the noun when it is the subject of the sentence, i.e. when the person or thing is performing the action of the verb. Thus, in our example above, "The dog chased the ball", it is "the dog" who is doing the chasing. The dog is the subject of the sentence, and so we use the nominative case. The nominative case is the one in which words are listed in dictionaries.

2.5 Personal pronouns

A pronoun is a word which is used instead of the noun in order to avoid tedious repetition. There are various kinds of pronouns; here, we are concerned only with personal pronouns. The sentence "John had a bath and then John dressed" seems odd, whereas "John had a bath and then he dressed" is less so because the personal pronoun "he" takes the place of "John". Personal pronouns are those which replace the names of people (as in our example) and of things – the cat (it); the book (it); the buildings (they).

Of course, we might say simply: "John had a bath and (got) dressed". Here, we don't actually use either the noun or the pronoun, but leave it to be understood that the person who dressed was the same person as had a bath. Czech is similar to English in this respect – it is not always necessary to use the pronoun when we want to express the idea that the same person is doing more than one thing.

The Czech personal pronouns are shown in the following table.

Singular		Plural	
I	**já**	we	**my**
you	**ty**	you	**vy**
he	**on**		**oni** or **ony**
she	**ona**	they	**ony**
it	**ono**		**ona**

IMITATED PRONUNCATION: (2.5): *yah; ti; on; o-na; o-no; mi; vi; o-n'yi; o-ni; o-ni; o-na.*

You will have noticed that there are various possible forms of "they". The first two are, as you will probably have realized, different forms for the masculine animate and inanimate. If all of the elements of the group comprising "they" are the same gender then, obviously, you don't have a problem. If not, the rules governing the form which is appropriate are complex. For the purposes of this course, and in practice in the Czech Republic, you need remember only that:

(a) you will always be understood if you use **oni**
(b) if there is just one masculine animate element in the group – for example, one man, three women and four girls – then the masculine animate form is used: if this strikes you as sexist, then ... that's how you remember the rule!
(c) **ona** is used very rarely – when it appears in the exercises below, it means "she", not "they" – but when doing the exercises – e.g. Exercise 2.2(c)(iii) – you should write in all the possibilities for "they".

At this point, we should mention an important point of etiquette which concerns the second person. In English, "you" is both a singular and a plural pronoun; in Czech, as you have seen above, there are different forms for the second person singular and plural. If you are speaking to someone you do not know well, you should use the plural form (**vy**) together with the plural form of the verb. You use **ty** only to people with whom you have an informal relationship, or to children.

2.6 The verb "to be" (být)

Verbs are words which are used to express what is happening – for example, "I am running", "He is eating", "She goes", "You will learn", "He flew". In these sentences, "am running", "is eating", "goes", "learn", "flew" are all verbs. In dictionaries, verbs are shown in their <u>infinitive</u> forms, i.e. in the form "to be", "to have", "to run", "to eat" etc. As you will have realized, verbs describe things that are happening now, things that have happened in the past and things that will happen in the future. The form of the verb varies according to whether the action <u>is</u> taking place, <u>was</u> taking place or <u>will</u> take place at some future time. This variation is what we call "tense" – the tense of the verb changes according to when the action happens. In this course, we will explain what each tense expresses as we meet it. For now, we are concerned with the present tense (what <u>is</u> happening now – as we speak or write). The following table shows the present tense of the verb "to be".

Singular		Plural	
I am	**jsem**	we are	**jsme**
you are	**jsi**	you are	**jste**
he is			
she is	**je**	they are	**jsou**
it is			

IMITATED PRONUNCIATION (2.6): *beet; sem; si; ye; sme; ste; so'u; nay-sem; nay-si; nay-sme; nay-nee.*

To say, "I am not", "you are not" and so on, you add **ne** to the forms given above. This is easy to remember: you are stating a <u>ne</u>gative. So, we have **nejsem** (I am not), **nejsi** (you are not), **nejsme** (we are not) and so on – with one exception. This is the third person singular (he is not, she is not, it is not) which is **není**. This is an irregularity: all languages have irregularities which simply have to be learned – and this is the first one you have encountered in Czech.

Now see how well you have grasped what you have learned by trying Exercise 2.2 in which you will need to use the personal pronouns, together with the verb "to be".

Exercise 2.2

In this exercise, we provide the personal pronouns – your job is to provide the correct form of the verb "to be" to go with them.

(a) First, the positive form of the verb:

(i) vy .... (ii) ty .... (iii) ona (feminine singular) ....
(iv) já .... (v) oni .... (vi) my ....

(b) Next, the negative form:

(i) já .... (ii) on .... (iii) vy .... (iv) my ....
(v) ty .... (vi) ono .... (vii) oni ....

(c) Now, provide the personal pronouns to agree with the form of the verb we have provided:

(i) .... jsme (ii) .... nejsou (iii) .... jsi (iv) ....
jsem (v) .... není (vi) .... je (vii) .... jste.

2.7 The verb "to have" (*mít*)

The following table shows the present tense of the verb "to have".

Singular		Plural	
I have	**mám**	we have	**máme**
you have	**máš**	you have	**máte**
he has			
she has	**má**	they have	**mají**
it has			

IMITATED PRONUNCIATION (2.7): *meet; mahm; mahsh; mah; mah-me; mah-te; mah-yee; ne-mahm; ne-mah-te.*

The negative (I have not; I do not have etc.) is formed in the same way as the negative of the verb "to be" – thus: **nemám** (I do not have), **nemáte** (you (plural) do not have) etc.

2.8 The reflexive (se)

When a verb is accompanied by **se**, it is said to be reflexive. This characteristic is found in many languages but seems odd and "foreign" to English speakers. "Reflexive" means "turning back on oneself" and this is exactly what reflexive verbs do. You can perhaps understand this best by deciding which of the following seems more natural to you: "I am getting ready for the journey" or "I am getting myself ready for the journey"; "He is preparing for bad news" or "He is preparing himself for bad news". Possibly you are hard put to decide. The difference between the two sentences in each case is the addition of "myself" and "himself". This is the reflexive pronoun: "myself" and "himself" refer, respectively, to "I" and "he" – to the same person. Other languages use this much more extensively than we do and in contexts that we might find surprising, since its addition, unlike our English examples above, can actually change the meaning of the other words. However, if we "think foreign", it begins to fit into place! Our first example uses it with the verb "to have". If you know that **jak** means "how", how would you translate **Jak máte?** If you replied, "how you have?", you would, of course, be correct. Now, what about **Jak se máte?** "How (do) you have yourself"? Well, literally, yes – but a Czech person would understand this as "How are you?" – not such a quantum leap, really. (If the person you were speaking to were a member of your family, or a close friend, you would use the singular form of "you" i.e. **Jak se máš.**)

Here are some more phrases using the reflexive **se** which you can use to reply to the question **Jak se máte?** or **Jak se máš?**

Mám se dobře	I'm fine
Mám se docela dobře	I'm quite well
Mám se velmi dobře	I'm very well
Mám se tak tak	So-so
Mám se nic moc	I'm alright (i.e. OK, nothing special either way)

IMITATED PRONUNCIATION (2.8): *yak; yak mah-te; yak se mah-te; yak se mahsh; mahm se dob-rzhe; mahm se dot-sel-a dob-rzhe; mahm se vel-mi dob-rzhe; mahm se tak tak; mahm se n'yits mots.*

Exercise 2.3

Complete the following sentences by filling in the form of **mít** *which is required by the pronoun in brackets. The first one is done for you.*

1 (on) Jak se .... ? **On** *means "he", so*: **Jak se má?**

2 (oni) Jak se .... ?

3 (ty) Jak se .... ?

4 (vy) Jak se .... ?

5 (ona) Jak se .... ?

Now provide answers to the question, "Jak se .... ?" by writing the correct form of **mít** *in the blank space. Again, the first one is done for you.*

6 (ona) .... se dobře.   (**Ona** *can mean "she" or "they", so your answer could be* **Má se dobře** OR **Mají se dobře**.)

7 (já) Ne .... se dobře.

8 (oni) .... se dobře.

9 (ty) .... se dobře.

10 (my) .... se dobře.

Exercise 2.4

(a) Complete the following dialogue. Assume that the two people have not known each other for long, and use the formal (2nd person plural) forms of the personal pronoun and verb.

A: Dobrý den.

B: ....

A: Jak se ....?

B: Děkuji, ...

A: Na shledanou.

B: ....

(b) In this dialogue, assume that the people have an informal relationship.

A: ....

B: Ahoj.

A: Jak ....?

B: ...., dobře. A ty?

A: Nic moc, ...

B: ....

A: ....

2.9 Adjectives

There are two types of adjective in Czech – <u>hard</u> adjectives and <u>soft</u> adjectives. There is no such distinction in English. Whether an adjective is hard or soft depends on its ending in the nominative singular form – i.e. the form in which you will find it in a dictionary. If the last letter is ý, then the adjective is hard; if the last letter is í, then it is soft. The two types of adjective are treated differently.

(a) *Hard adjectives*
Hard adjectives change their endings according to the
gender of the noun to which they apply. In dictionaries, the
masculine form is the one which is shown. The word for
"new" is **nový**. **Nový** is a hard adjective. Watch how its
endings change according to the nouns it is describing:

Masculine	nový den	new day
Feminine	nová káva	new coffee
Neuter	nové ráno	new morning

So, to form the feminine and neuter forms, you remove the
ý. This gives you the stem **nov-** to which you add á if the
noun is feminine, or é if the noun is neuter.

Let's try this with **dobrý** which means "good". Removing
the ý leaves us with the stem **dobr-**. Coffee is a feminine
noun, so we add á to the stem: **dobrá káva**. And what about
"good morning"? This was one of the greetings you learned
earlier.

(b) *Soft adjectives*
You'll be pleased to read that the form of the soft adjectives
is the same in all genders. Thus:

Masculine	moderní dům	modern house
Feminine	moderní dívka	modern girl
Neuter	moderní auto	modern car

IMITATED PRONUNCIATION (2.9): *nov-ee; nov-ee den; nov-ah
kah-va; nov-eh rah-no; dob-ree; dob-rah kah-va; mod-er-n'yee doom;
mod-er-n'yee d'yeev-ka; mod-er-n'yee ow-to.*

2.10 Possessive pronouns

As its name suggests, a possessive pronoun indicates
ownership. Possessive pronouns, therefore, express the
concept of "<u>my</u> book", "<u>their</u> dog" and so on. As ownership
is always "of" <u>something</u> (i.e. of a noun), you will find that
the grammar systems of some languages refer to them as
"possessive adjectives". In Czech, although they are treated
as part of the system of pronouns, you will be able to detect

a kinship with the adjectives which will help you with the pattern of the endings.

In English, these possessive words do not change, whether we are referring to "my daughter" (who is feminine), "my son" (who is masculine), or "my car" (which is neuter). This is not so in Czech: as with the adjectives, the form of the pronoun varies according to the gender of the noun. Look carefully at the following table, and then we'll work through a couple of examples together.

	Masculine	Feminine	Neuter
my	**můj**	**má**	**mé**
your	**tvůj**	**tvá**	**tvé**
his	**jeho**	**jeho**	**jeho**
her	**její**	**její**	**její**
its	**jeho**	**jeho**	**jeho**
our	**náš**	**naše**	**naše**
your	**váš**	**vaše**	**vaše**
their	**jejich**	**jejich**	**jejich**

IMITATED PRONUNCIATION (2.10, reading across, omitting repeats): *moo'y, mah, meh; tvoo'y, tvah, tveh; ye-ho; ye-ee; ye-ho; nahsh, nash-e; vahsh, vash-e; ye-yikh.*

Using the above table, let's work out how we would say, "our house". The first thing we must do is find the gender of the noun. The word for "house" is **dům** which is a masculine noun. Looking under the masculine column for "our" we find **náš**, so "our house" translates as **náš dům**. Not as easy as English, but not difficult either – rather like working out a puzzle based on logic. No other example is any more difficult – but you have to keep a clear head, particularly with examples such as "his mother" where the pronoun is quite clearly one gender and the noun another. We'll work this one out in the same way.

(a) Find the noun and its gender first (**matka**: feminine)
(b) Then, look across from "his" to the feminine column (**jeho**).

And what about "my pen"?

(a) Find the noun and its gender first (**pero**: neuter)
(b) Then, look across from "my" to the neuter column (**mé**).

2.11 Interrogative pronouns

Interrogative pronouns are the words we use to ask
questions about people or things.

Kdo	Who?
Co	What?
Jaký, -á, -é	What sort of ... ?

To ask, "Who is that?", you would say **Kdo je to?** We shall
meet **to** in the next paragraph, but it also means "that", in
the sense of the word "that" which is being used here. **Je**
shouldn't have been a problem – it's the third person
singular of the verb "to be". Now imagine that you've seen a
dish of food in a shop window and want to know what it is.
What would you say?

You will have noticed that there are three forms of **jaký**.
The endings are the same as the adjective endings we were
using above. This tells us that, when we want to ask, "What
sort of .... ?", we need to know the gender of the noun and
to use the appropriate form of **jaký**:

Jaký muž?	What sort of man?
Jaká žena?	What sort of woman?
Jaké auto?	What sort of car?

The reply you receive is likely to be in the form of adjectives
– a tall man, a pretty woman, a fast car. These adjectives
must agree with the nouns. Look at the following question
and responses.

Jaký muž?	**Vysoký muž**	A tall man
Jaká žena?	**Hezká žena**	A pretty woman
Jaké auto?	**Rychlé auto**	A fast car

IMITATED PRONUNCIATION (2.11): *k'do; tso; yak-ee, yak-ah, yak-eh;*
k'do ye to; yak-ee muzh; yak-ah zhen-a; yak-eh ow-to; vi-so-kee muzh;
hes-kah zhen-a; rykh-leh ow-to.

The following exercise will show you how well you've grasped this business of making sure that the endings of your adjectives and possessive pronouns agree with the noun to which they relate. Remember that your starting-point should always be the gender of the noun. The exercise isn't difficult, but you will have to be careful! Take it slowly – it's all very new to you at this stage. Remember that, if you do things correctly, people will understand you, even if you are a little slow, and most will be willing and able to help you if you go wrong or get stuck. But if you confront them with something that is so slapdash that they have difficulty working out what it is you are <u>trying</u> to say, then saying it more quickly will add to, not lessen, their problem.

Exercise 2.5

Translate the following into Czech, using the correct form of the possessive pronouns and adjectives. Remember that the adjective given in brackets is in the masculine form – all we have done is provide what you would find in a dictionary; you must still work out how it changes (if at all) in each example.

1 Our new house.   (nový)

2 His big book.   (velký)

3 Their modern apartment. (moderní)

4 My clean window.   (čistý)

5 Your (s.) white coffee. (bílý)

6 Her beautiful table.   (krásný)

7 Their foreign car.   (cizí)

2.12 Demonstrative pronouns

These are the pronouns which we use to indicate or single out one person or thing from a group. For example, if we were to say "That is a beautiful painting", we would be pointing to one painting in particular. "That" is the demonstrative pronoun. Likewise, when we say "This is a good play", we are talking about a particular play – the one we are seeing now. "This" is the demonstrative pronoun. By now, you will probably not be surprised to learn that the forms of the demonstrative pronoun change according to the gender of the noun (the person or thing) being referred to.

In the nominative case, the demonstrative pronouns take the following forms.

Masculine	**ten**
Feminine	**ta**
Neuter	**to**

So

Ten muž	This/that man
Ta káva	This/that coffee
To auto	This/that car

Now look at these two sentences: "That house is new"; "That is a new book". The first falls four-square within the situation we have just been describing; **dům** (house) is a masculine noun, and this sentence would therefore be translated as **Ten dům je nový**. In the second sentence, though, "that" is not as closely related to "book", but is used more in the sense of "the thing I am indicating". In this situation, **to** is used <u>whatever</u> the gender of the noun. (But **nový** must of course still agree with the noun.) Thus: **To je nová kniha.**

IMITATED PRONUNCIATION (2.12): *ten; ta; to; ten muzh; ta kah-va; to ow-to; ten doom ye nov-ee; to ye nov-ah k'ne-ha.*

In colloquial speech, many Czech speakers make more use of pronouns than we do in English. This is partly to compensate for the fact that Czech does not draw the distinction between "the" and "a" as English does. If I say to you,

"I am going to buy a book", I may or may not have a particular book in mind. But if I say, "I am going to buy the book",
then clearly I am referring to a specific title and, furthermore, I am assuming that you know what it is. "The" refers
to one known or identifiable person or thing, whereas "a"
could be any one of the type of thing I am talking about.
Czech does not have separate words for "the" and "a", and
this "gap" is filled by the demonstrative pronouns **ten, ta**
and **to**. To make even more of a point of the person or thing
being singled out, you will find the basic **ten, ta, to** elaborat-
ed as shown below. As you can see, these changes are not
affected by gender – they are simply tacked onto the
pronoun. Don't try to commit this table to memory: you will
be understood if you use the basic pronouns we've just
learned. If you are able to use some of the forms below, then
your Czech will sound more colloquial, but that isn't something you need worry about at this stage. We have included
them here because you will hear them being used by others.

Gender	This/that (often used when we would use "the")	This (i.e. this particular one rather than another of the same type; used in formal situations)	This here (as in preceding column, but in informal situations)	That there (used to highlight a contrast between two people or things or when what is referred to is some way away)
Masculine	ten	**tento**	ten**hle**	**tam**ten
Feminine	ta	**tato**	ta**hle**	**tam**ta
Neuter	to	**toto**	to**hle**	**tam**to

Exercise 2.6

The following dialogue includes a noun and two hard adjectives. These three words are in bold type. Study the conversation carefully.

A:	Kdo je to?	Who is that?
B:	To je **student**.	That is a **student**.
A:	Jaký je ten student?	What sort of student (is that)?
B:	To je **dobrý** student.	(That is) a **good** student.

OR

B:	Ten student je **dobrý**.	That student is **good**.
A:	Je ten student **mladý**?	Is that student **young**?
B:	Ano, je.	Yes, he is.

Now construct dialogues on the same pattern, using the following groups of noun and two adjectives. In each case, the adjectives are hard adjectives but we have shown them here with the endings which agree with the noun with which we have asked you to use them – but don't forget that you will also need the appropriate form of **jaký**.

(a) **dítě** (child);   **malé** (small);   **hodné** (good)

(b) **dívka** (girl);   **vysoká** (tall);   **mladá** (young)

(c) **doktor** (doctor);   **český/Čech** (Czech);   **dobrý** (good)

What gender is each of these nouns? Although the "rough guide" in paragraph 2.2 applies to all of them, notice how the adjective ending is another guide to the gender of the noun.

Now do the same thing with the next three: don't forget that your first question will be "What is that?" rather than "Who is that?"

(d) **okno** (window);   **velké** (big);   **čisté** (clean)

(e) **židle** (chair);   **stará** (old);   **hezká** (pretty)

(f) **park** (park);   **velký** (big);   **krásný** (beautiful)

2.13 Surnames

The words for Mr, Mrs and Miss are **pan, paní** and **slečna** respectively. In Czech, surnames have a masculine and a feminine form. This is not difficult and can be summarized in these two rules:

(a) if the masculine form of the name ends in **-ý**, that **ý** is replaced by an **á** in the feminine form
(b) in all other cases, you simply add **-ová** onto the masculine form to make the feminine.

Applying these two rules in turn, then, the Černý family may consist of:

pan Černý	Mr Černý
paní Černá	Mrs Černý
slečna Černá	Miss Černý

while the Novák family would be:

pan Novák	Mr Novák
paní Nováková	Mrs Novák
slečna Nováková	Miss Novák

IMITATED PRONUNCIATION (2.13): *pan; pan-ee; sletch-na; cher-nee; cher-nah; nov-ahk; nov-ah-ko-vah.*

2.14 Nationality

Again, the feminine form differs from the masculine but shouldn't cause us any great problem: the most usual way of forming the feminine is to add **-ka** to the masculine. Here are a few examples:

Angličan	Englishman	**Angličanka**	Englishwoman
Američan	American man	**Američanka**	American woman
Rakušan	Austrian man	**Rakušanka**	Austrian woman

with a couple of important exceptions:

Němec	German man	**Němka**	German woman
Čech	Czech man	**Češka**	Czech woman

2.15 Professions

The same applies to professions as to nationalities. Look at the following examples:

lékař	**lékařka**	doctor
stevard	**stevardka**	air steward/stewardess
student	**studentka**	student
inženýr	**inženýrka**	engineer
učitel	**učitelka**	teacher

and a couple of important exceptions:

právník	**právnička**	lawyer
úředník	**úřednice**	official/clerk

IMITATED PRONUNCIATION (2.15): *leh-karzh (-ka); ste-vart (-ka); stu-dent (-ka); in-zhe-neer (-ka); u-chit-el(-ka); prahv-n'yeek; prahv-n'yeech-ka; oo-rzhed-n'yeek; oo-rzhed-nits-e.*

2.16 Dialogue

Finally, here is a short dialogue in Czech. Before you look at the translation which is given below, see how much of the dialogue you can understand. Because it's quite a simple dialogue, and some of the words are very similar to their English equivalents, you would probably be able to guess its overall meaning even if you didn't genuinely understand it. By all means read through it quickly for the general sense, but then go through it again more thoroughly. Make sure you know the meaning of every single one of the words used. Not just the words which convey the gist of the conversation, but all the little ones as well. If you make a habit of doing this in the early stages of the course, you will find it easier to understand passages which contain more words in total, but fewer whose meanings are obvious!

DIALOGUE

A: Dobrý den.

B: Dobrý den.

A: Jak se máte?

B: Děkuji, dobře. A vy?

A: Velmi dobře, díky. Kdo je ta mladá žena?

B: To je nová studentka.

A: Je Američanka?

B: Ne, Angličanka.

A: A kdo je ten mladý muž?

B: To je Petr.

A: Je taky Angličan?

B: Ne, je Čech.

TRANSLATION

A: Good morning (or afternoon).

B: Good morning (or afternoon).

A: How are you?

B: Fine, thanks. And you?

A: Very well, thanks. Who's that young woman?

B: She's a new student.

A: Is she American?

B: No, she's English.

A: And who's that young man?

B: That's Peter.

A: Is he English, too?

B: No, he's Czech.

As a test of how well you understand the Czech, try to answer the following questions. Don't guess – give reasons for your answers, based on the form of the words used in the Czech text.

Exercise 2.7

1   How well do you think A and B know each other?

2   If the words **žena** and **muž** had not been included, we would still have known the sexes of the students A was asking about. How?

Chapter 3

3.1 Nouns: accusative case

When a noun is in the accusative case, the person or thing is the <u>direct object</u> of the action of the verb. Do you remember our sentence, "The girl patted the dog" from paragraph 2.3? If not, turn back now and read that paragraph again. Here are two more examples: "Mrs Jones kicked her car"; "I like Prague". Can you say which noun is the subject and which the object of each sentence? If you can't, you might well find that you've informed a Czech speaker that Mrs Jones' car kicked her and that Prague likes you. Here's an easy way to tell them apart:

the <u>subject</u> is the noun which is <u>carrying out</u> the action of the verb;

the <u>object</u> is the noun which is <u>receiving</u> the action of the verb.

Applying this to the second sentence, then, we have one noun (Prague) and a pronoun (I) which, remember, stands in for a noun – in this case, my name. It is "I" who am doing the liking, so "I" am the subject of the sentence, and your pronoun would be in the first person singular, nominative case (can you remember the Czech word?). Prague, on the other hand, isn't doing anything. It is the <u>object</u> of my liking, and so you would use the accusative form of the noun "Prague". After this example, Mrs Jones and her car should be easy: Mrs Jones is doing the kicking, so Mrs Jones is the subject (nominative case) whereas the car isn't doing anything except <u>receiving</u> kicks from Mrs Jones, i.e. it is the <u>object</u> of her kicking (accusative case).

The changes in ending from nominative to accusative forms fall into broad patterns according to:

(a) <u>gender</u>
(b) whether the noun is <u>hard</u> or <u>soft</u>

The following table shows how some of the words you have learned already in their nominative forms change their endings when they are in the accusative case.

	Hard		Soft	
Gender	Nom.	Acc.	Nom.	Acc.
Masc. animate	student	studen**ta**	muž	muž**e**
Masc. inanimate	most	most	pokoj	pokoj
Fem. ("a" or "e" ending)	žena	žen**u**	židle	židl**i**
(consonant ending)	místnost	místnost	skříň	skříň
Neuter	město	město	moře	moře
("i" or "e" ending)	náměstí	náměstí	děvče	děvče

IMITATED PRONUNCIATION (3.1, reading across, omitting repeats): *stu-dent, stu-dent-a; muzh, muzh-e; most; pok-oy; zhe-na, zhe-nu; zhid-le, zhid-li; meest-nost; skrzheen'y; mn'yes-to; mor-zhe; nah-mn'yes-t'yee; d'yef-che.*

Look at the table carefully and note where and how the ending of the noun changes for the accusative case. Look back at the table of common noun endings in paragraph 2.2 and compare the grouping in that table with the patterns in this one. The examples in that table are all in the nominative case: as you look at them, try to work out how you would change them if the nouns were the direct object of the verb.

As yet, we have taught you only two verbs, so the sentences you can make are necessarily very simple and artificial-sounding but, so that you become accustomed to thinking about the possible need to change the form of the noun when you speak or write Czech, try the following exercise.

Exercise 3.1

Translate the following sentences into Czech.

1   Mrs Novák has a textbook.

2   The Englishman has a girlfriend.

3   We have an apartment.

4   That lady has a rose.

5   She does not have a chair.

3.2 Adjectives: accusative case

Adjectives must "agree" with the nouns they are describing. We have already seen how hard adjectives in the nominative case agree with the <u>gender</u> of the noun (paragraph 2.9).

The <u>case</u> of the adjective must also agree with the noun to which it applies so, if the noun is in the accusative case, then the adjective which is describing that noun must also be in the accusative case. Let's take **velký** (big; large) as our hard adjective example here, and **moderní**, once again, as our soft adjective. (Can you remember the nominative singular forms of **velký** for each gender?) The following table shows the accusative forms alongside the nominative ones you know already.

	Hard		Soft	
Gender	Nom.	Acc.	Nom.	Acc.
Masc. animate	velký	velk**ého**	moderní	modern**ího**
Masc. inanimate	velký	velký	moderní	moderní
Feminine	velká	velk**ou**	moderní	moderní
Neuter	velké	velké	moderní	moderní

IMITATED PRONUNCIATION (3.2, reading across, omitting repeats): *vel-kee, vel-keh-ho; mod-er-n'yee, mod-er-n'yee-ho; vel-kah, vel-koh; vel-keh.*

Now try Exercise 3.2. If you made any mistakes in Exercise 3.1, you will be able to consolidate your corrections; if you got all of Exercise 3.1 correct, then "well done", and all you've got to worry about here is the adjectives!

Exercise 3.2

Translate into Czech.

1 Mrs Novák has a new textbook.

2 The Englishman has a young girlfriend.

3 We have a clean apartment.

4 The lady has a beautiful rose.

5 She does not have a large chair.

3.3 Personal pronouns: accusative case

English too can change its forms according to case. Consider the following sentences: "The mother bathed the child and put the child to bed". You should be happy now with the idea that "the child" is the direct object in this sentence – it is the child who is affected by the mother's actions of bathing and putting to bed. However, to make the sentence sound natural, we need a pronoun in place of "the child", so we say "The mother bathed the child and put her/him to bed", not "put she/he to bed". Here are the Czech and English personal pronouns in both the nominative and accusative cases.

Singular				Plural			
Nom.		Acc.		Nom.		Acc.	
I	**já**	me	**mě (mne)**	we	**my**	us	**nás**
you	**ty**	you	**tě (tebe)**	you	**vy**	you	**vás**
he	**on**	him	**ho, jej**		**oni**		
			(jeho animate only**)**	they	**ony**	them	**je**
she	**ona**	her	**ji**		**ona**		
it	**ono**	it	**ho, jej, je**				

IMITATED PRONUNCIATION (3.3, accusative): *mn'ye, (mn'e); t'ye, (te-be); ho, yay, (ye-ho); yi; ho, yay, ye; nahs; vahs; ye.*

The pronouns which are enclosed in brackets are long forms which are used when the speaker wishes to emphasize the pronoun. At this stage, this is not something you should worry about, since you are more likely to hear these forms than to have to use them.

As between **jej** and **ho** (masculine and neuter), **jej** is the more colloquial.

Again, the fact that we haven't yet done any work on verbs means that we are limited in the sentences that we can give you to translate, but the next short exercise will give you a little practice in using the accusative form of the personal pronouns. To make this a little more challenging, we have included some revision on noun genders (the more often you have to make the conscious effort to decide the gender of a noun, the more quickly you will learn to recognize them).

Exercise 3.3

Translate into Czech. Where a noun is given [in square brackets], do not put the noun itself into the accusative case, but use the appropriate form of the personal pronoun. For example:

Do you have it [the book]? *In English, the correct pronoun for "the book" is, of course, "it"; but "book" in Czech is* **kniha,** *which is a feminine noun. The correct pronoun in Czech, therefore, is* **ji,** *so you would translate this as* **Máte ji?**

1 Does she have them?

2 Do you (*plural, or formal singular*) have it [the coffee]?

3 Do we have it [the house]?

4 Does he have it [the chicken]?

5 Does she have it [the table]?

6 Does he have it [the bicycle]?

3.4 Possessive pronouns: accusative case

In Chapter 2, we looked at the possessive pronouns which accompany nouns when the nouns are in the nominative case, and you now know how to differentiate between "my house", "your house", "their house" and so on (**můj dům, tvůj dům, jejich dům** etc.). When we've covered the accusative case, you'll be able to make up sentences where the object owned is the direct object of the sentence – such as "He has my pen"; "I have your book".

The following table shows how the form of the possessive pronouns changes from the nominative to the accusative case. You will notice that there is no change in any of the third person forms: **jeho** and **jejich** never change (they remain the same in each of the seven cases); **její** happens to be the same in the accusative case as it is in the nominative, but it does take different forms in other cases, as you'll

discover later. Of the two forms given for the feminine first
and second persons singular, the first is the more colloquial.

Do you see any similarities between the changes between
the nominative and accusative cases in this table and those
in the table of adjectives in paragraph 3.2?

	Masculine		Feminine		Neuter	
	Nom.	Acc.	Nom.	Acc.	Nom.	Acc.
my	můj	(animate): **mého** (inanimate): **můj**	má	**moji/mou**	mé	**moje**
your	tvůj	(animate): **tvého** (inanimate): **tvůj**	tvá	**tvoji/tvou**	tvé	**tvoje**
his	jeho	jeho	jeho	jeho	jeho	jeho
her	její	její	její	její	její	její
its	jeho	jeho	jeho	jeho	jeho	jeho
our	náš	**našeho**	naše	na**ši**	naše	naše
your	váš	**vašeho**	vaše	va**ši**	vaše	vaše
their	jejich	jejich	jejich	jejich	jejich	jejich

IMITATED PRONUNCIATION (3.4, reading across, inanimate
following animate, words/endings in bold type): *meh-ho, moo'y;
mo-yi, moh; mo-ye; tveh-ho, tvoo'y; tvo-yi, tvoh; tvo-ye; nash-e-ho; nash-i;
vash-e-ho; vash-i.*

Even though we still don't have any verbs in our vocabulary,
knowing the accusative case of the possessive pronouns
adds significantly to the range of things we can say, and
we're going to practise them in Exercise 3.4. As before,
there's nothing in this exercise that we haven't covered, but
you must focus your attention carefully. Before checking
your answers, ask yourself the following questions:

(a) have I used the correct <u>case</u> for each of the nouns?
(b) do any pronouns and/or adjectives used in connection
    with the noun agree with it (i) in gender and (ii) in case?

This exercise draws on a number of the topics we've covered so far, and you may well find it challenging – at least that's what we hope! Don't be put off by this, don't rush, and remember that you're not competing with anyone. Take it slowly, and go over your answers carefully before checking them. There are one or two words here that you have not yet met: you will find them in the vocabulary section at the end of the lesson.

Exercise 3.4

1   I have her book.

2   He has their room.

3   You (plural, or formal singular) have our bicycle.

4   She has a new pen.

5   Do you have my book?

6   They have a new flat. Their new flat is not clean.

7   My brother has my table; I have his chair.

8   His girl has a pretty rose.

9   Doesn't she have my bag?

10 Our town has a large square.

How did you get on? If you did make mistakes, go back over what we've done. Don't just check that the key answer really <u>was</u> right, but work out why you made the mistake you did. Pretend that someone else made the mistake, and try to explain to them exactly how it was they went wrong.

3.5 Reflexive possessive pronoun

This is not something to which you need give a great deal of attention at this stage. We've included it here for two reasons: first, you may well come across it either in speech or in writing; second, it gives a precision in meaning which

English lacks, so you may find it useful if the forms of the possessive pronoun which you have learned so far leave the Czech speaker in some doubt as to who actually owns the item to which you are referring. Let us explain.

Consider the sentence, "Karel gave Petr Karel's book". This, of course, sounds unnatural – an ideal candidate for the use of a pronoun (which would, obviously, be "his"). Similarly, "Mr and Mrs Smith gave Mr and Mrs Brown Mr and Mrs Smith's key" is very cumbersome – more natural would be "Mr and Mrs Smith gave Mr and Mrs Brown <u>their</u> key." But can you see a problem with this? When the pronouns are substituted, it is not one hundred percent clear <u>whose</u> book or key is being given. The truth of the matter is usually clear from the context, or we would ask for clarification if we were in doubt, but the fact remains that, when the sentence stands alone, it can be understood in more than one way.

Here's another ambiguity which can arise in English: "I am taking my book back to the library". Here, the book does not really <u>belong</u> to the speaker – it is not "my" book but the library's book. And what about, "He was late because his train was delayed"? Strictly speaking, this is also inaccurate because the train does not <u>belong</u> to him – it was simply the train on which he was travelling.

Czechs cover themselves in such situations by using the reflexive pronoun. Its effect is to make clear that the owner of the article following the pronoun is the subject of the sentence, i.e. the person or thing which is in the nominative case. It is often translated as "my own", "your own", "his own" etc. You will doubtless be pleased to learn that, although you must still make sure that the gender of the reflexive pronoun agrees with the noun which follows it, the pronoun itself does not change regardless of whether we are talking about "my (own)", "your (own)", "our (own)" etc.

In form, it is virtually the same as the possessive pronouns we have already covered. You are more likely to meet or to need it in the accusative case, but we have shown it below in the nominative and in the accusative.

Gender of noun	Nominative	Accusative
Masculine animate	**svůj**	**svého**
Masculine inanimate	**svůj**	**svůj**
Feminine	**svá**	**svou**
Neuter	**své**	**své**

We are not going to do an exercise on this, since it falls into the category of "very-useful-to-know-but-not-necessary-to-say", but we'll just give one example to show you the difference between the possessive pronouns you've learned and the reflexive possessive pronoun we've just looked at. Here are two sentences.

Karla má její auto.
Karla má své auto.

Both translate literally as "Karla has her car" but, whereas the first leaves some doubt about whether the car belongs to Karla or to some other female, the second makes it clear that the car in question is Karla's own car.

We're not going to labour this particular point, but you may find that you want to come back to this section if you find yourself in a situation where you want to make the identity of the owner of an object absolutely clear.

IMITATED PRONUNCIATION (3.5): *svoo'y, sveh-ho; svoo'y, svoo'y; svah, svoh; sveh, sveh; kar-la mah yay-yee ow-to; kar-la mah sveh ow-to.*

3.6 Demonstrative pronouns: accusative case

In paragraph 2.12, we explained how all of the forms of the demonstrative pronoun derive from the basic forms **ten**, **ta** and **to**. The table below shows how these basic forms change from the nominative to the accusative case.

Gender	Nominative	Accusative
Masculine animate	ten	**toho**
Masculine inanimate	ten	ten
Feminine	ta	**tu**
Neuter	to	to

The next table shows how the other accusative forms are developed from the ones above. Compare the way in which they are made up with the table in paragraph 2.12. As you can see, when the case changes, it is **ten**, **ta** and **to** which change, the endings for the other forms remaining the same in each of the seven cases.

Gender	This/that (often used when we would use "the")	This (i.e. this <u>particular</u> one rather than another of the same type; used in formal situations)	This here (as in preceding column, but in informal situations)	That there (used to highlight a contrast between two people or things, or when what is referred to is some way away)
Masculine animate	toho	toho**to**	toho**hle**	**tam**toho
Masculine inanimate	ten	ten**to**	ten**hle**	**tam**ten
Feminine	tu	tu**to**	tu**hle**	**tam**tu
Neuter	to	to**to**	to**hle**	**tam**ten

3.7 Cardinal numbers

Cardinal numbers are those which describe a specific number of things (one, two, three and so on); listed below are the numbers 1–20. Ordinal numbers are those which describe the position of something relative to others (for example, "He came third in the race"; "She was the first off the boat"), and we'll deal with them in a later lesson. Notice how, if you concentrate on learning the numbers 1–10, you'll find it easy to count from 11–20 since all you do, with only very slight modifications (see how easily you can spot them), is to add **-náct** to the numbers you already know.

jeden	one	**jedenáct**	eleven
dva	two	**dvanáct**	twelve
tři	three	**třináct**	thirteen
čtyři	four	**čtrnáct**	fourteen
pět	five	**patnáct**	fifteen
šest	six	**šestnáct**	sixteen
sedm	seven	**sedmnáct**	seventeen
osm	eight	**osmnáct**	eighteen
devět	nine	**devatenáct**	nineteen
deset	ten	**dvacet**	twenty

Notice, too, the word for "twenty" – it doesn't end in **-náct**, true, but does anything else about it strike you? If not, write down the figures 2 and 20 one underneath the other, then write down the Czech words for them in the same way. Recognizing patterns like this will save you a great deal of time, and may even let you have a stab at something you haven't consciously learned, in a situation where you would otherwise be stuck.

You should, of course, try to learn these numerals as well as you can but, for practical purposes, it would make sense to concentrate on one to ten. After all, numbers are international and there are a number of ways round situations which involve them. For example, you can explain that you don't understand Czech (**Nerozumím česky**) and ask the person to write it down for you (**Napište mi to, prosím**). Or, if you are specifying the quantity yourself, you can write it down.

IMITATED PRONUNCIATION (3.7): *yed-en; dva; trzhi; chuht-ir-zhi; p'yet; shest; sed-uhm; oss-uhm; dev-yet; des-set; yed-en-ahtst; dva-nahtst; trzhin-ahtst; chuht-uhrn-ahtst; pat-nahtst; shest-nahtst; sed-uhm-nahtst; oss-uhm-nahtst; dev-a-ten-ahtst; dvat-set.*

3.8 Cardinal numerals: gender

Jeden and **dva** have different forms for the feminine and neuter:

	Masculine	Feminine	Neuter
one	**jeden**	**jedna**	**jedno**
two	**dva**	**dvě**	**dvě**

but the other numerals take the same form (i.e. as shown in paragraph 3.7) in all genders.

3.9 Cardinal numbers: case

Yes, numbers do change (slightly) according to the case of the nouns they precede. But the good news is that the only one we need deal with at this stage is **jeden**. All the others remain as listed above whether the noun is in the nominative or accusative case. Again, taking a practical view, if you can say the basic form of the number correctly, you will be understood – although it's nice to be impressive as well as comprehensible! Here, then, are the nominative and accusative forms of **jeden**.

Masculine		Feminine		Neuter	
Nom.	Acc.	Nom.	Acc.	Nom.	Acc.
	(animate):				
jeden	jed**noho**	jedna	jed**nu**	jedno	jedno
	(inanimate):				
	jeden				

Vocabulary

asi	maybe; perhaps (*also*: about; some; something like)
byt (*m*)	flat; apartment
dlouho	a long time
doma	at home
fotografie (*f*)	photograph

jenom	only
pokoj (*m*)	room
postel (*f*)	bed
sám	alone
stačí	enough
štěstí (*n*)	luck; happiness
tady	here
taška (*f*)	bag
vedle	beside; next to
velmi	very
volný	free; vacant; loose

IMITATED PRONUNCIATION (3, vocab): *a-si; bit; dloh-ho; do-ma; fo-to-gra-fi-ye; yen-om; pok-oy; pos-tel; sahm; sta-chee; sht'yes-t'yee; ta-di; tash-ka; ved-le; vel-mi; vol-nee.*

3.10 Dialogue

As with the dialogue in Chapter 2, read the Czech through quickly for the gist of the conversation but, before looking at the translation, work through it carefully word by word. When doing so, make a mental note of anything which you realize you missed, or misunderstood, on your initial run-through. You should then compare your translation with the first translation provided. This should match your own almost exactly. If it doesn't, identify the points of difference and check that you understand why it was different. If necessary, work back through the relevant paragraphs. You will notice that the English of the first translation is stilted – how a non-English speaker might translate into newly learned English. Compare the second translation: the meaning is the same, but it is English as we would actually speak it. In the following lessons we will provide only one translation – a colloquial one. Until you feel confident in translating from Czech straight into colloquial English, go through the stages described above: Czech → literal translation of the Czech into English → English-as-it-would-be-spoken. (You will find the words with which you are unfamiliar in the Vocabulary section.)

DIALOGUE

A: Tady je učebnice.

B: Jaká (učebnice)?

A: Česká. Máš svou českou učebnici?

B: Ne, nemám. Mám ji doma. Ta není moje. Je asi jeho.

A: Tady je fotografie. Je tam dům a to je Petr.

B: Ano, tam má Petr svůj byt. Není velký, ale je hezký. Nemá ho dlouho. Má tam jenom postel, velký stůl, moderní židli a starou skříň.

A: To stačí, ne? Má štěstí, že má svůj byt.

B: Ale Petr tady není sám. Kdo je ta mladá žena vedle?

A: To je jeho přítelkyně Helena.

B: Je velmi hezká.

TRANSLATION 1

A: There's a textbook here.

B: What sort of (textbook)?

A: A Czech one. Do you have your Czech textbook?

B: No, I do not. I have it at home. It's not mine. It may be his.

A: There is a photograph here. There is a house and it is Petr.

B: Yes, Petr has his flat there. It's not large, but it's nice. He does not have it long. He has only a bed, a big table, a big table, a modern chair and an old wardrobe there.

A: That's enough, isn't it? He is lucky to have his flat.

B: But Petr is not alone. Who is the young woman next to (him)?

A: It is his girlfriend, Helena.

B: She's very pretty.

TRANSLATION 2

A: There's a textbook here.

B: What sort of textbook?

A: A Czech one. Have you got yours (Czech textbook)?

B: No, I haven't. I've got it at home. That one's not mine. It might be his.

A: There's a photograph here. It's of a house, and Petr's in it.

B: Yes, Petr's flat's there. It's not big, but it's nice. He hasn't had it long. He's only got a bed, a big table, a modern chair and an old wardrobe in it.

A: That's enough, isn't it? He's lucky to have his own flat.

B: But Petr's not by himself. Who's the young woman next to him?

A: It's his girlfriend, Helena.

B: She's very pretty.

Chapter 4

- *Progress note*
- *Verbs: present tense of **dělat** and other verbs in the first conjugation*
- *Irregular verbs*
- *Negatives*
- *Prepositions taking the accusative and prepositional verbs*
- *Pronunciation of prepositions*
- *The family and marital status*

4.1 Progress note

You should be proud of the fact that your knowledge of Czech already extends beyond the "noun-and-point-with-finger" stage.

Think about what you have achieved so far:

- you know two of the most important verbs – **být** (to be) and **mít** (to have);

- you have begun to build up your vocabulary of nouns and, furthermore, you can distinguish between, say, "my book", "the book", "that book" and so on;

- you can qualify these nouns with adjectives;

- you can do all of these things <u>grammatically</u>

– and that's not counting surnames, nationality, professions, and numbers.

As you learn the basic grammatical structures and get to

grips with the verbs, you'll find that you can express your-self correctly in a rapidly expanding range of situations. Increasingly, all you need to do is to look up words in the dictionary to extend your vocabulary according to your needs – <u>because you know how to make those words perform the function required.</u>

4.2 Verbs: present tense of *dělat* (to do; to make)

Every sentence requires a verb; the more verbs you know, the less restricted will be your use of the language. Regular Czech verbs fall into one of four patterns (called "conjugations" by grammarians), and we shall look at each of those patterns in turn. For the moment, we will deal only with the present tense – i.e. that tense which expresses <u>what is happening now.</u>

For the first conjugation, we are going to take the verb **dělat** as our model. The pattern here applies to all verbs whose infinitive ends in **-at** or **-át** . The present tense of **dělat** is shown in the following table. Study it carefully and note how there is a common <u>stem</u> and different <u>ending</u> for each person. Establish what the stem is (clue: this isn't as foregone a conclusion as it might appear at first glance – be careful!) and then underline the endings.

Singular		Plural	
I do *or* make	**já dělám**	we do *or* make	**my děláme**
you do *or* make	**ty děláš**	you do *or* make	**vy děláte**
he does *or* makes	**on**		
she does *or* makes	**ona dělá**	they do *or* make	**oni dělají**
it does *or* makes	**ono**		

If you have written down your stem as **dělá-** , LOOK AGAIN. Look at the third person plural!

Now write down the endings for each person. Do it neatly, in the form of a chart. Now turn back to paragraph 2.7 and do <u>exactly</u> the same with the table you find there.

Here are some more verbs which follow this pattern:

čekat	to wait
dívat se	to look at
hledat	to look for; to seek
hlídat	to watch; to guard
obědvat	to have lunch
odpovídat	to answer/reply (to questions)
otvírat	to open
poslouchat	to listen to; to obey (e.g. one's parents)
prodávat	to sell
snídat	to have breakfast
trhat	to pick (e.g. flowers, fruit etc.)

So, to conjugate these verbs, you first find the stem and then add the appropriate ending to that stem.

IMITATED PRONUNCIATION (4.2): *d'yel-at; yah d'yel-ahm; ti d'yel-ahsh; o-na d'yel-ah; mi d'yel-ahm-e; vi d'yel-aht-e; o-ni d'yel-a-yee; chek-at; d'yee-vat se; hle-dat; hlee-dat; ob'yed-vat; od-pov-ee-dat; ot-veer-at; pos-loh-khat; prod-ah-vat; snee-dat; tr-hat.*

4.3 Meanings of the present tense

In the table above, we gave the English form of the present tense as "I do", "you do", and so on. This form, however, is only one of the ways we have in English of describing "what is happening now" – literally, at the moment of speaking. There is another form which is used to describe actions which are happening now <u>and continuing:</u> "I am doing", "you are doing", "we are making" etc. Bear this in mind: you <u>do</u> know how to say "I am (doing something)"!

Exercise 4.1

So that you can check that you have understood how to find the stem and add the endings, try writing out the present tense of **prodávat** *(to sell). If, when you compare it with the Key, you made any mistakes, try again with one of the other verbs given above. Remember that they all work in exactly the same way – this is what is meant by a "regular" verb.*

When you have managed to conjugate one of the verbs completely correctly, then move on to the next exercise.

Exercise 4.2

Translate into Czech. In questions 5–8, use the appropriate demonstrative pronoun to express "the". In questions 3, 5 and 6, put **na** *between the verb and the noun: you will understand why when you have worked through paragraph 4.8.*

1 We are looking for a house.

2 I am selling the car.

3 She looks at the sea.

4 They look for the official.

5 The girl answers the question.

6 You (*pl*) are watching the man; he is having breakfast.

7 You (*s*) are having lunch; is it chicken?

8 The (male) teacher listens to the girl.

4.4 Irregular verbs

The verbs listed in 4.2 above are all <u>regular</u> verbs, which means that they follow the pattern laid down for their conjugation; learn that pattern, and you've mastered the lot. <u>Irregular</u> verbs (which occur in every language, including English) don't conform to any pattern, and each one has to be learned individually when you need to use it. The extent of the irregularity can, of course, vary – from a change in the ending for only one particular person in the conjugation to a conjugation that looks nothing like any of the regular patterns. Look for similarities whenever you can find them. If you can be aware that an irregular verb is basically the same as, say, **dělat**, but with a change in the third person singular, then that makes your task easier than treating the entire verb as a whole new unit of learning. We have, in fact, met one irregularity already – remember **není**, "he/she/it is <u>not</u>"?

4.5 Words associated with time

Learn these three useful words – you'll need them in the next exercise:

ted'	now, nowadays, at present
často	often
také	also

IMITATED PRONUNCIATION (4.5): *ted'y; chas-to; ta-keh.*

Exercise 4.3

Fill in the correct form of **dělat**.

1 Co ted' vy ....

2 Ne .... oni to také?

3 Já to často ne ....

4 Ty to .... ?

5 Co tady on .... ?

6 My tady ne .... ?

4.6 Negatives

You will remember that forming negatives – i.e. "I do not", "you are not making" etc. – is easy. You simply add **ne-** before the positive form of the verb. To re-cap on this, try the following exercise.

Exercise 4.4

1 They are not looking for the bag.

2 I am not selling the bicycle.

3 She is not opening the door.

4 We do not make the thing.

5 He does not sell books.

6 You (*pl*) do not look for the station.

7 You (*s*) do not pick the fruit.

4.7 Prepositions

Prepositions have many functions. For our purposes, it is sufficient to know that, as their name suggests, they are words which indicate position. For example, in the following three sentences the underlined words are prepositions; they tell us what the relationship or connection is between the two nouns "book" and "table":

The book is <u>on</u> the table. The book is <u>under</u> the table. The book is <u>near</u> the table.

The use of a preposition can affect the case of the noun which follows it and, in the paragraphs which follow, we are going to introduce the prepositions after which the noun must take the accusative case.

These are as follows:

na
to	
in	(when motion is implied, i.e. when "in" is used in the sense of "into")
at	(when "at" carries the implication of "towards", e.g. "He is looking at the horizon.")
on	(whenever "on" could be replaced by "onto", e.g. "I am putting the coal on the fire.")
upon	(and "for" when used in the sense of "upon", e.g. "I am waiting for the train.")

přes   across

pro   for

mimo   outside; besides

za
within	(when applied to a span of time, e.g. "The concert starts in ten minutes.")
for	

4.8 Prepositional verbs

Think for a moment about how we use the verb "to wait".

The sentence, "I am waiting" doesn't really tell us anything. The "waiting" is always <u>for</u> something or someone – a letter, a bus, a friend – or Godot. In the sentence, "I am waiting for the flight to be called", "waiting" and "for" together make up what is called a prepositional verb.

When a prepositional verb occurs in Czech, you must be careful to use the correct case for the noun or pronoun with which it is connected. Unfortunately, when a prepositional verb, such as **čekat na** (wait for) occurs, the personal pronouns in the accusative case take a different form.

Look back now at the table in paragraph 3.3.

j becomes **n** and **e** becomes **ě**

Using the table in paragraph 3.3, let's work through a couple of examples.

You (formal)	are waiting	for	him.
Vy	**čekáte**	**na**	**něho.**

BUT

I	am waiting	for	you.
Já	**čekám**	**na**	**vás.**

stays exactly the same as it would have done and is no problem.

4.9 Pronunciation: more about stress

You learned in paragraph 1.2 that the stress in Czech is always on the first syllable of the word – i.e. **pr<u>á</u>ce** (work; job); **<u>šk</u>ola** (school); **<u>ži</u>dle** (chair). However, if there's a one-syllable preposition in front of the word, the stress goes on the preposition, which is then pronounced altogether with the word to which it relates. Thus: **<u>do</u> práce** (to work); **<u>ve</u> <u>šk</u>ole** (at school); **<u>na</u> <u>ži</u>dli** (on the chair).

IMITATED PRONUNCIATION (4.9): *prah-tse; shko-la; zhid-le; dop-rah-tse; vesh-ko-le; nazh-id-li.*

4.10 The family

Here are the Czech words for the most common members of a family. As well as acquiring new vocabulary, pay some attention to the endings of the words. As the gender follows the "natural" gender (i.e. mother is feminine, etc.), you won't need to make a conscious effort to work them out. What you can do is to use these words to help you familiarize yourself with the typical endings of each gender so that, when you come across an inanimate object, you will be more practised in recognizing the gender without looking it up.

rodina	family
jméno	name
příjmení	surname
rodiče	parents
otec	father
matka	mother
dcera	daughter
syn	son
bratr	brother
sestra	sister
strýc	uncle
teta	aunt
manželka; žena	wife
manžel; muž	husband

Note also:

táta	dad
tatínek	daddy
máma	mum
maminka	mummy

IMITATED PRONUNCIATION (4.10): *rod-yin-a; meh-no; pr'zheey-men-yee; rod-i-che; o-tets; mat-ka; tser-a; sin; bra-tr; ses-tra; streets; tet-a; man-zhel-ka, zhen-a; man-zhel, moozh; tah-ta; tat-ee-nek; mah-ma; mam-ink-a.*

4.11 Marital status

svobodný	single
rozvedený	divorced

Note that **svobodný** (single) and **rozvedený** (divorced) are adjectives. As they end in **ý**, they are hard adjectives and so the ending will differ depending on whether you are referring to a male or a female.

"Married" differs totally according to whether we are talking about a man or a woman.

On je ženatý	He is married
Ona je vdaná	She is married

Depending on your sense of humour, this is quite amusing: does the word **žena**tý bring to mind any of the other words you have learned?

Exercise 4.5

You are going to describe some of the members of the Novák family. Don't forget what you learned in paragraph 2.13.

1   Mr Novák is married.

2   Mrs Novák is married.

3   Mr and Mrs Novák are parents.

4   The family is a mother, a father, a brother and a sister.

5   The brother is divorced; his name is Karel. (use reflexive verb for "his name is")

6   The sister is married; her name is Jana.

7   The brother does not obey the parents.

8   The old aunt is single. Mrs Novák is her sister.

Vocabulary

ale	but
dveře (*f*)	door
i	even
jméno (*n*)	name
jmenovat se	to be called
myslíš	do you think? (**Myslet** is a third conjugation verb; the third conjugation is dealt with in Chapter 6.)
obchodník	businessman
otázka (*f*)	question
ovoce (*n*)	fruit; fruits
práce (*f*)	job
šťastná	happy
studuje	she studies (**Studovat** is a second conjugation verb; the second conjugation is dealt with in Chapter 5.)
věc (*f*)	thing
všechno	everything; all
zajímavý	interesting
zboží (*pl*)	goods
znát	to know

IMITATED PRONUNCIATION (4, vocab): *al-e; dverzh-e; i; meh-no; men-o-vat-se; mis-leesh; ob-khod-neek; ot-az-ka; ov-ot-se; prahts-e; sht'yast-nah; stud-oo-ye; v'yets; f'shekh-no; za-yee-mav-ee; zbo-zhee; znaht.*

4.12 Dialogue

Remember to work through the steps described in paragraph 3.10.

DIALOGUE

A: Znám jednoho anglického studenta. Ted' studuje tady.
B: Myslíš Petera.
A: Ano! Znáš ho?
B: Často na něho čekám. Znám také jeho rodinu.
A: Co dělají jeho rodiče?
B: Jeho otec je obchodník. Prodává i české zboží. Jeho matka je právníčka. Také jeho sestra studuje právo.
A: Má jen jednu sestru?
B: Má jednu sestru a jednoho bratra. Ale bratr už je ženatý a má malé dítě, syna Jonathana. Ted' on a jeho manželka hledají nový byt. Ale co dělá tvá sestra?
A: Má ted' novou zajímavou práci. Je šťastná!

TRANSLATION

A: I know an English student. He is studying here now.
B: Do you think it's Peter? (It couldn't be Peter, could it?)
A: Yes! Do you know him?
B: I often wait for him. I know his family too.
A: What do his parents do?
B: His father's a businessman. He even sells Czech goods. His mother's a lawyer. His sister's studying law too.
A: Has he just one sister?
B: He has a sister and a brother. But his brother is already married and has a small child, Jonathan. At the moment, he and his wife are looking for a new flat. But what does your sister do?
A: She has an interesting new job. She's happy!

Chapter 5

- *Verbs: present tense of **studovat** and other verbs in the second conjugation*
- *Nouns, adjectives and pronouns in the genitive case*
- *Quantities, weights and measures*
- *Prepositions taking the genitive*
- *Days of the week*

5.1 Verbs: present tense of *studovat* (to study)

We now come to the second conjugation. The pattern shown below for **studovat** applies to all the regular verbs whose infinitive ends in **-ovat**. You will notice that there are two possible endings for the first person singular and for the third person plural. The first ending is used in formal situations and in written communications, the second in informal, spoken contexts. As with the formal and informal forms of "you", we recommend that you concentrate on learning the first (formal) ending.

As before, work out what the stem is and underline the endings.

Singular		Plural	
I study	**já studuji** OR **já studuju**	we study	**my studujeme**
you study	**ty studuješ**	you study	**vy studujete**
he studies she studies it studies	**on ona studuje ono**	they study	**oni studují** OR **oni studujou**

Other verbs which follow this pattern include:

cestovat	to travel
děkovat	to thank (remember **děkuji?**)
investovat	to invest
kupovat	to buy
lyžovat	to ski
malovat	to paint
milovat	to love
ohrožovat	to threaten
opakovat	to repeat; to revise
pečovat	to take care of; to tend
pěstovat	to grow; to cultivate; to breed
plánovat	to plan
potřebovat	to need
pracovat	to work
připravovat	to prepare
privatizovat	to privatise
telefonovat	to telephone
vyslovovat	to pronounce

Exercise 5.1

Fill in the correct form of **studovat.**

1   My .... tady.

2   Co ona .... ? Medicínu?

3   Ano, a také oni .... medicínu.

4   Ty už ne .... ?

Now try applying the **studovat** *pattern to the verb given before each group of questions.*

pracovat
5   Vy .... tady?

6   Ne, tady .... Petr, ale my .... tamhle.

potřebovat
7   Vy .... tuto knihu.

8   Já ji ne ...., ale oni ji ....

milovat
9   To je hezký svetr! Já .... tuto barvu.

10 Matka .... starou hudbu.

ohrožovat
11 Oni .... přirodu.

12 Jejich politika .... mír.

kupovat
13 Co .... (ty)?

14 .... (já) kávu.

15 Ale ona už .... kávu.

telefonovat
16 Kdo .... ?

17 Petr a Marie ted' ....

18 Ty ne .... ?

Exercise 5.2

Translate into Czech.

1   I need a meal.

2   The man is buying a car.

3   We are growing a beautiful new rose.

4   They are buying a large wardrobe.

5   I love her daughter.

6   You do not need the book, but you are buying it.

7   We are repeating the song.

8   Are you (*plural*) studying the grammar?

9   Don't you (*singular*) love Miss Novák?

10   They thank ["you" is implied here] very much.

5.2 Nouns: genitive case

This case is used when there is an element of <u>possession</u> or <u>belonging</u> surrounding the noun. By now, you should have no difficulty in identifying the subject and direct object in a sentence such as "They like the car". Now, what about "They like the colour of the car"? The verb is "like"; it is they who are doing the liking, so "they" is the subject of the sentence; it is the colour which is on the receiving end of the liking, so "colour" is the direct object – but where does that leave "of the car"? The answer is: in the genitive case!

Another way of saying the same thing would have been, "They like the car's colour". The presence of an apostrophe is thus another signal that the genitive case should be used.

You'll remember from paragraph 3.1 that the endings depend on:

(a) <u>gender</u>
(b) whether the noun is <u>hard</u> or <u>soft</u>

The following table shows the nouns in the genitive case in relation to their nominative forms.

Gender	Hard		Soft	
	Nom.	Gen.	Nom.	Gen.
Masc. animate	student	student**a**	muž	muž**e**
Masc. inanimate	most	most**u**	pokoj	pokoj**e**
Fem. ("a" or "e" ending)	žena	ženy	židle	židle
(consonant ending)	místnost	místnosti	skříň	skříně
Neuter	město	města	moře	moře
("i" or "e" ending)	náměstí	náměstí	děvče	děvče**te**

5.3 Genitive case: special groups of masculine inanimate nouns

Some hard masculine inanimate nouns take the same form as the masculine animates, i.e. they take an **a** ending rather than a **u** ending. These groups are as follows:

(a) days of the week: Thursday (**čtvrtek**) and Friday (**pátek**) are masculine
(b) most of the months of the year
(c) some proper names (e.g. **Mělník** is **Mělníka** in the genitive)
(d) nouns expressing some sort of geographical location:

kout	corner	**kouta**
ostrov	island	**ostrova**
les	forest	**lesa**
domov	home	**domova**

(e) some other nouns which cannot be conveniently grouped, e.g.:

sýr	cheese	sýra
oběd	lunch	oběda
večer	evening	večera
chléb	bread	chleba

Exercise 5.3

Connect the following nouns using the genitive case, and translate the result into English.

Example:	**dům; žena**	house; woman
	dům ženy	the woman's house (*literally,* "the house [of] the woman")

1   obraz; Praha

2   okno; pokoj

3   budova; pošta

4   ovoce; ostrov

5   číslo; autobus

6   kniha; student

7   plán; město

8   fotografie; přítelkyně

9   auto; přítel

10 láhev; víno

5.4 Genitive case: quantities, weights and measures

Although the element of possession is absent from expressions such as "many books", "a little coffee", "a kilo of sugar" and so on, these are nonetheless instances in which the genitive is required. If this seems confusing at first, the key word is "of" – whether used expressly as in "a kilo of sugar", or implied as in "a little coffee". Think of the latter as "a little [of the available] coffee", "many [of the available] books" etc.

Words for a small quantity are **trochu** and **málo**; words for a large quantity are **hodně** and **mnoho**.

Exercise 5.4

As in Exercise 5.3, connect the pairs of words by using the genitive case, and then translate into English.

1   kousek; sýr

2   sklenice; víno

3   láhev; pivo

4   kousek; máslo

5   kus; chléb

6   trochu; cukr

7   hodně; voda

8   mnoho; práce

9   málo; čas

10 šálek; káva

5.5 Prepositions taking the genitive case

Prepositions were explained in paragraph 4.7, where you learned that, when certain prepositions occurred, the noun which followed them took the accusative case. Nouns following the prepositions below take the genitive case:

z, ze	from; out of
do	to; into
od	from

bez	without
u	at
vedle	next to
kromě	apart from; except
vyjma	as **kromě**, but more formal
blízko	near

5.6 Pronunciation: single-letter prepositions

Like the one syllable prepositions in paragraph 4.9, single-letter prepositions (which include **s**, **v**, and **k** – which we will meet later – as well as **z** from the list above) are also pronounced as one with the words they go with, but they cannot bear the stress themselves because they have no vowel with which to create their own syllable. Thus: **s bratrem** (with a brother); **v domě** (in the house); **k domu** (towards a house); **z domu** (from a house).

5.7 Adjectives: genitive case

We are going to follow the same pattern here as in paragraph 3.2 where we explained that adjectives have to agree with their nouns in <u>gender</u> and in <u>case.</u> So, if we want to say "the tall girl's house" (i.e. the house of the tall girl), "girl" will be in the genitive case and so the adjective "tall" must also be in the genitive. Here are the adjectives in the nominative and the genitive cases.

	Hard		Soft	
Gender	Nom.	Gen.	Nom.	Gen.
Masc. animate	velký	velk**ého**	moderní	modern**ího**
Masc. inanimate	velký	velk**ého**	moderní	modern**ího**
Feminine	velká	velk**é**	moderní	moderní
Neuter	velké	velk**ého**	moderní	modern**ího**

At this point, you may think that the similarities between cases are more of a hindrance than a help! (For example, **velké** denotes neuter in the nominative and accusative cases, but feminine in the genitive.) Don't forget that, translating from Czech, you'll always have the noun to help you – the adjective just tags along with it, agreeing for agreement's sake. For translating into Czech, one suggestion would be to copy out the tables onto index cards, marking the endings as we've done, and keeping them in front of you as you translate – they won't become familiar overnight but, as you use them, you'll gradually find that you've known the correct form before you look at your card to check it.

Exercise 5.5

Each question consists of a noun qualified by an adjective. Precede each pair with either **mnoho** *or* **hodně** *(many; much) or* **málo** *or* **trochu** *(few; little) – which means, of course, that both the noun and the adjective will have to take the genitive case.*

1   indický čaj

2   černá káva

3   dobré maso

4   čerstvá zelenina

5   pražská šunka

6   cizí zelenina

7   zahraniční ovoce

Exercise 5.6

Now translate the following sentences into Czech.

1 We work from morning to evening.

2 It is a map of Prague.

3 I need a lot of sugar.

4 I have only a little soup.

5 It is a nice picture of Prague castle.

6 There is only a little salt here.

5.8 Personal pronouns: genitive case

In paragraph 5.2, we considered the sentence, "I like the colour of the car". If the conversation about the car had been going on for some time, the speaker might have said instead, "I like the colour of it." Here "it" is standing in place of "the car". As the car was in the genitive case, the pronoun representing it must take the genitive case. Other examples would include, "He didn't like the look of her"; "He heard the sound of me approaching"; "Just the thought of them was enough".

The following table shows the genitive forms of the personal pronouns in comparison with the nominative forms.

Singular				Plural			
Nom.		Genitive		Nom.		Genitive	
I	**já**	of me	**mě (mne)**	we	**my**	of us	**nás**
you	**ty**	of you	**tě (tebe)**	you	**vy**	of you	**vás**
he	**on**	of him	**ho/jej**		**oni**		
she	**ona**		**(jeho** animate only**)**	they	**ony**	of them	**jich**
it	**ono**	of her	**jí**		**ona**		
		of it	**ho/jej**				

As with the personal pronouns in the accusative case, the longer forms in brackets are used:

(a) when the speaker wishes to put emphasis on the pronoun – for example, in "I won't ask <u>him</u>" (where the implication is that "he" is the last person you would ask), the pronoun would move to the beginning of the sentence: **Jeho se neptám**.

(b) after prepositions (see paragraph 5.9 below).

5.9 Pronouns preceded by a preposition

When a pronoun comes after a preposition, the rule in paragraph 4.8 applies:

j → n;   **e → ě**

Examples:

"Without him": "without" is **bez**; bez is a preposition taking the genitive; the genitive form of "him" is "jeho" but changes because of the preposition it changes to **něho**.

"Next to her": "next to" is **vedle**; vedle is a preposition taking the genitive; the genitive form of "her" is "jí" but because of the preposition it changes to **ní**.

5.10 Prepositional verbs in relation to the genitive case

The following reflexive verbs indicate that the object will take the genitive and not the accusative case:

bát se	to be afraid [i.e. to be afraid <u>of</u>]
	(1st per. sing. = **bojím se**)
ptát se	to ask [i.e. to ask <u>of</u>]
účastnit se	to take part in; to participate [i.e. to be a part <u>of</u>]

Remember that **se** never changes (see paragraph 2.8).

Exercise 5.7

Put the pronouns given in brackets into the genitive case.

1   Jedete bez (oni).

2   To děláš jen kvůli (já).

3   Kromě (já) tam jedou všichni.

4   Ten test je těžký; jistě se (on) bojí.

5   Zeptáš se (oni) nebo (ona)?

6   (On) se neptám.

Exercise 5.8

In the blank spaces, fill in personal pronouns to take the place of the nouns in brackets.

1 Ptáš se (bratra) nebo (sestry)? Ptáš se .... nebo ....

2 Kdo sedí vedle (Jany)? Kdo sedí vedle .... ?

3 Bojí se (paní Nováková) .... ?

4 Jistě si nevšimne (auto) ....

5 Neúčastníme se (maratón) ....

6 Tam je (Petr a jeho přítelkyně), ale kdo sedí vedle .... ?

5.11 Possessive pronouns: genitive case

Remember the rules on agreement: if a noun is in the genitive case, then any possessive pronoun accompanying it must also be in the genitive. Actually, this is the old "the pen of my aunt" chestnut! "The pen of my aunt" is, of course, an awkward way of saying, "my aunt's pen", and it is expressions such as this for which you need the possessive pronouns in the genitive case. Have a look at the table below, in which the genitive forms are compared with the nominative, and then we'll work through an example.

| | Masculine | | Feminine | | Neuter | |
	Nom.	Genitive	Nom.	Genitive	Nom.	Genitive
my	můj	**mého**	má	**mé**	mé	**mého**
your	tvůj	**tvého**	tvá	**tvé**	tvé	**tvého**
his/its	jeho	jeho	jeho	jeho	jeho	jeho
her	její	její**ho**	její	její	její	její**ho**
our	náš	**naše**ho	naše	naší	naše	naše**ho**
your	váš	**vaše**ho	vaše	vaší	vaše	vaše**ho**
their	jejich	jejich	jejich	jejich	jejich	jejich
reflexive	svůj	sv**ého**	svá	sv**é**	své	sv**ého**

Just for the sake of it, then, let's use "my aunt's pen" as our example. The reason many foreign speakers come up with "the pen of my aunt" is that this actually is the structure used in their own language. Czech is one of those languages, so you might find it useful at first to re-phrase expressions which involve a genitive case noun with a possessive pronoun into that format. Getting to grips with our example, then, we shall assume that your aunt's pen is the subject of the sentence – notice that it is the <u>pen</u> which is the subject and thus takes the nominative case (**pero**). This leaves us with the "of my aunt" bit. As the pen <u>belongs</u> to "my aunt" (is <u>of</u> my aunt), it should be obvious from what you have learned already about the genitive case that "aunt" will take the genitive (**tety**). The possessive pronoun "my" must agree with the noun in number, case, and gender: as you can see from the table above, this is **mé**. So, "my aunt's pen" is **pero mé tety**.

Exercise 5.9

Now you try! The following sentences all involve possessive pronouns in the genitive case. If you need to, carry out the intermediate step we explained above when we re-worked the colloquial "my aunt's pen" into "the pen of my aunt".

1   My brother's name.

2   My sister's car.

3   The colour of your (singular) chair.

4   The door of our house.

5   Is this your book? No, this is my brother's book.

5.12 Demonstrative pronouns: genitive case

If this is your first experience of learning a language in which case affects the form of the nouns, adjectives and pronouns, you may well find your mind glazing over as you confront table after table of different forms. Think of the language as a logic puzzle in which you reach the solution by drawing inferences from the pieces of information supplied. Applied to your learning of Czech, the function of the noun in the sentence is your starting-point; once you know that, and assign a case to it, then all of the adjectives and various types of pronouns take that case too, thus building up a sentence which is your "solution". The table below consists of a comparison between the nominative and the genitive forms of the demonstrative pronouns: don't try to learn it – there's no point in doing so because, on its own, it serves no useful function. What you <u>should</u> do is make sure you understand <u>when</u> you should use the genitive and make a brief note of the differences between the two forms given. With practice, you will find that you need to refer back to the table less and less frequently.

First, then, the basic forms:

Gender	Nominative	Genitive
Masculine animate	ten	**toho**
Masculine inanimate	ten	**toho**
Feminine	ta	**té**
Neuter	to	to**ho**

The next table shows the development of the other forms of the Czech demonstrative pronouns. As there is nothing irregular about this, you might like to try to draw up your own table before looking at ours.

Gender	This/that (often used when we would use "the")	This (i.e. this particular one rather than another of the same type; used in formal situations)	This here (as in preceding column, but in informal situations)	That there (used to highlight a contrast between two people or things, or when what is referred to is some way away)
Masculine	toho	toho**to**	toho**hle**	**tam**toho
Feminine	té	té**to**	té**hle**	**tam**té
Neuter	toho	toho**to**	toho**hle**	**tam**toho

Exercise 5.10

Again, we should emphasize that you are very likely to hear these expressions, but you will not have to use them yourself. Translate the following short dialogue into English.

A: Bojím se toho člověka.

B: Tohohle?

A: Ne. Tamtoho.

B: Aha! Tohoto.

5.13 Days of the week

Note that in Czech these don't start with a capital letter:

neděle (f)	Sunday	čtvrtek (m)	Thursday
pondělí (n)	Monday	pátek (m)	Friday
úterý (n)	Tuesday	sobota (f)	Saturday
středa (f)	Wednesday		

Could you provide the genitive forms of Thursday and Friday correctly? (Look back at paragraph 5.3.) Now try this short exercise in which you will have to use some of the possessive and demonstrative pronouns.

Exercise 5.11

In sentences 1–4, put the words in brackets into their correct form. Sentences 5–8 should be translated into Czech.

1 Kromě (můj manžel) tam pracuje i má známá.

2 Bez (tvůj přítel) tam nejdeme.

3 Vedle (ten dům) je velké parkoviště.

4 Vyjma (ten nový student a ta nová studentka) jsou všichni tady.

5 There is a large department store next to our house.

6 It's that pretty girl's book.

7 Everybody's there except our (male) friend.

8 It is my firm's address.

Vocabulary

adresa *(f)*	address
autobus *(m)*	bus
barva *(f)*	colour; paint; dye
bojí se	he/she/it is afraid of (**Bát se** is irregular as it conjugates as a third conjugation verb; third conjugation verbs are dealt with in Chapter 6.)
budova *(f)*	building
cukr *(m)*	sugar
čaj *(m)*	tea
čas *(m)*	time
čerstvý	fresh
číslo *(n)*	number
člověk *(m)*	person
hrad *(m)*	castle
hudba *(f)*	music
indický	Indian
kousek *(m)*	small piece

kus *(m)*	piece; bit; chunk; lump
jedete	you go (This is the second person plural of **jet**; the verbs of motion are covered in Chapter 7.)
jen	only; just (genitive: jenom)
jistě	certainly; surely
kvůli	because of; for the sake of
láhev *(f)*	bottle
mapa *(f)*	map
maratón *(m)*	marathon
maso *(n)*	meat
máslo *(n)*	butter
nebo	or; otherwise
obchod *(m)*	firm; business
obchodní dům *(m)*	department store
obraz *(m)*	picture
parkoviště *(n)*	car-park
pěkný	nice
pivo *(n)*	beer
píseň *(f)*	song
plán *(m)*	plan; schedule; design
polévka *(f)*	soup
politika *(f)*	politics; policy
poradce *(m)*	advisor
pošta *(f)*	post-office; post; mail
Praha *(f)*	Prague
příroda *(f)*	nature
sedí	he/she/it sits (**Sedět** is a third conjugation verb; these are dealt with in Chapter 6.)
sklenice *(f)*	glass
sůl *(f)*	salt (genitive: soli)
svetr *(m)*	sweater; jumper; pullover
šálek *(m)*	cup
šunka *(f)*	ham
také	also; too
test *(m)*	test
těší mě/(mne)	pleased to meet you
těžký	difficult; hard; heavy
už	already; now; yet
víno *(n)*	wine
voda	water

všichni	all; everybody
všímat si	to notice; take notice
zahraniční	foreign
zelenina (*f pl*)	vegetables

5.14 Dialogue

DIALOGUE

Petr: Já jsem Petr Novák.

Ivana: Já jsem Ivana Černá.

Petr: Těší mě.

Ivana: Těší mě.

Petr: Jak se máte?

Ivana: Děkuji, docela dobře.

Petr: Vy tady pracujete?

Ivana: Ano, pracuji jako poradce v bance.

Petr: Jsem rád, že jsem v Praze.

Ivana: Ano, Praha je hezké město.

TRANSLATION

Petr: I am Petr Novák.

Ivana: I am Ivana Černá (Black).

Petr: Pleased to meet you.

Ivana: Pleased to meet you.

Petr: How are you?

Ivana: I'm well, thank you.

Petr: Are you working here?

Ivana: Yes, I work as an adviser in the bank.

Petr: I'm pleased to be in Prague.

Ivana: Yes, Prague is a fine city.

Chapter 6

- *Verbs: present tense of **mluvit** and other verbs in the third conjugation*
- *Irregular verbs*
- *Months of the year*

6.1 Verbs: present tense of *mluvit* (to speak)

The pattern shown below for **mluvit** applies to all the regular verbs whose infinitive ends in **-it** or **-et** or **-ět**, and so, as you can imagine, it covers a very large number of verbs. Because there are three possible infinitive endings for this conjugation, the stem of **mluvit** is **mluv-,** even though í is common to all persons.

Singular		Plural	
I speak	**já mluvím**	we speak	**my mluvíme**
you speak	**ty mluvíš**	you speak	**vy mluvíte**
he speaks	**on**		
she speaks	**ona mluví**	they speak	**oni mluví**
it speaks	**ono**		

Other verbs which follow this pattern include:

bát se	to be afraid
končit	to finish
ležet	to lie
myslet	to think; to suppose
nosit	to wear; to carry
prosit	to ask
sedět	to sit
slyšet	to hear
účastnit se	to take part in; to participate
učit	to teach
učit se	to learn
vidět	to see
zdravit	to greet

Exercise 6.1

The following short dialogue contains a number of blanks which you should fill in with the correct form of **mluvit**.

A: Kdo .... ? Jana?

B: Ne, ona ....

A: Vy .... anglicky?

B: Ano, my .... anglicky ale já .... také německy.

A: Můj syn .... také německy.

Exercise 6.2

Translate into Czech.

1　They are greeting the American woman.

2　Where do you see it?

3　Jana is asking for fruit. (Use **o** for "for" here.)

4　They are sitting over there.

5　You always carry a heavy bag.

6　I think she is beautiful.

7　He thinks it is an easy test.

8　What do you hear?

9　Where is the book lying?

10　Now she is teaching English in Prague.

6.2 Irregular verbs

As the third conjugation is so large, it is hardly surprising that it includes a fairly large number of irregular verbs. Two of these are very simple:

rozumět　　to understand
přicházet　to come

Their irregularity is only in the third person plural; in all the other persons, the **mluvit** pattern applies but, when you come to "they understand" and "they come", the ending is **-ějí**. So:

Já rozumím; ty rozumíš, ona rozumí, my rozumíme, vy rozumíte
BUT: oni rozumějí

and

Já přicházím, ty přicházíš, ona přichází, my přicházíme, vy
přicházíte
BUT: oni přicház**ejí**

6.3 The irregular verb *jíst* (to eat)

Jíst really is an irregular verb of the first order! Its infinitive
doesn't end in **it**, **et**, or **ět** but its endings have a strong
similarity to those of the third conjugation. Look carefully
at the table below.

Singular		Plural	
I eat	**já jím**	we eat	**my jíme**
you eat	**ty jíš**	you eat	**vy jíte**
he eats	**on**		
she eats	**ona jí**	they eat	**oni jedí**
it eats	**ono**		

Two points to note here:

(a) the stem consists only of **j**
(b) the endings are regular third conjugation endings apart
from the third person plural – **jedí**

6.4 The irregular verb *vědět* (to know)

Although this has a familiar-looking infinitive ending, it is
irregular because:

(a) the stem consists only of **v**
(b) the endings are regular third conjugation endings apart
from the third person plural – **vědí**

Look:

Singular		Plural	
I know	**já vím**	we know	**my víme**
you know	**ty víš**	you know	**vy víte**
he knows	**on**		
she knows	**ona ví**	they know	**oni vědí**
it knows	**ono**		

As we pointed out in paragraph 4.4, there is no polite way of saying that irregular verbs (in whatever language) are anything other than a pain in the neck, which is why we are introducing them gradually throughout the course instead of simply putting *irreg.* beside an infinitive and leaving you to sort it out on your own. But there are ways in which you could organize things so as to keep on top of it. One suggestion would be to keep a 5" x 3" card index box in which to file the irregular verbs in alphabetical order, with a brief note about the nature of their irregularity. This would allow you very quickly to check whether a verb was irregular or not. Another way of going about this would be to compile a list in the following format:

Verb	Conj. patt.	Notes
jíst (to eat)	3	stem "j" only; 3rd person plural: jedí
přicházet (to come)	3	3rd person plural: přicházejí
rozumět (to understand)	3	3rd person plural: rozumějí
vědět (to know)	3	stem "v" only; 3rd person plural: vědí (cp. jíst)

By doing this, adding to it as soon as you come across an irregular verb, and by giving it attention whenever you suspect that the verb you want to use might be irregular, they will gradually become second nature – a "Ready Reckoner" which you make yourself is far more valuable than a list prepared by somebody else.

Exercise 6.3

Fill in the gaps with the correct form of the verb given in bold.

1 **přicházet**   Oni už .... ? Oni ještě ne, ale on ....
                  Já .... až teď'.

2 **vědět**   Vy to .... ? My to ne ...., ale on to
                  jistě ....

3 **rozumět**   On už docela ...., ale oni ještě tak ne
                  .... Ty .... ? Ne, já ne ....

4 **jíst**   Oni už .... ? Ano, ale my ještě ne ....

5 **vědět**   Já ...., že je to pro tebe těžké.

6 **rozumět**   Ale už .... ?

6.5 Note on the use of pronouns with verbs

Although Czechs will use pronouns far more than we do in order to emphasize the person or thing they are talking about, don't forget that the different verb endings incorporate the pronouns so as to make clear <u>who</u> is carrying out the action. If you do not wish to make a particular point of this, then you don't need to use the pronoun itself – nor should you be surprised to <u>hear</u> the verb forms on their own: this is not a sign either of sloppy speech, or of informality.

Exercise 6.4

Answer the following questions with the correct forms of the verb, answering first in the affirmative, but then saying that someone else does not do the action in question. (Note that not all of the verbs belong to the third conjugation, so you will have to determine which conjugation they do belong to before adding the endings.)

1 Rozumíš?   Ano, ..., ale ona ....

2 Studují?   Ano, ..., ale my ....

3 Pracuje tady?   Ano, ..., ale oni tady ....

4 Mluvíte česky?   Ano, ..., trochu, ale oni ....

5 Už jedí?   Ano, ..., ale on ještě ....

6 Děláte to?   Ano, ..., ale ty to ještě ....

7 Víte to?   Ano, ..., ale oni to ....

8 Přicházejí často?   Ano, ..., ale já často ....

9 Jíš zeleninu?   Ano, ..., ale vy ....

10 Už končíme?   Ano, ..., ale oni ještě ....

6.6 Months of the year

Unlike English, these do not begin with a capital letter:

leden	January	**červenec**	July
únor	February	**srpen**	August
březen	March	**září**	September
duben	April	**říjen**	October
květen	May	**listopad**	November
červen	June	**prosinec**	December

All the months of the year are masculine except **září**, which is neuter. Do you remember what paragraph 5.3 said on this subject?

Vocabulary

lehký   easy
příliš   either; too
vždycky   always; at all times

6.7 Dialogue

DIALOGUE

A: **Mluvíte česky?**

B: **Ano, ale jenom trochu.**

A: **Rozumíte dobře?**

B: **To je velký problém – rozumím velmi málo.**

A: **Já také příliš nerozumím.**

TRANSLATION

A: Do you speak Czech?

B: Yes, but only a little.

A: Do you understand [it] well?

B: It's a big problem – I understand very little.

A: I don't understand all that much either.

Chapter 7

- *Verbs: present tense of* **číst** *and other verbs in the fourth conjugation*
- *Verbs of motion (**jít** and **jet**)*

7.1 Verbs: present tense of *číst* and other verbs in the fourth conjugation

The infinitives of the group to which **číst** belongs include those ending in **-íst, -ést, -ít, -ét, -ůst, -ást**, and **-ýt**.

Your best plan of action, when trying to decide which conjugation a verb belongs to, is to start by eliminating the first, second and third conjugations as possibilities before going on to treat the infinitive as a fourth conjugation verb. Be particularly careful to distinguish between **-et, -ět** (both third conjugation) and **-ét** (fourth conjugation) and between **-it** (third conjugation) and **-ít** (fourth conjugation).

Once you have done this, the endings follow the pattern below. Note how the **-ís** of the infinitive is dropped out, leaving the stem as **-čt-** – **t** does not belong to the endings. Bearing in mind what we said above in paragraph 6.5, we have given only the verb forms for each person and have left out the personal pronoun.

Singular		Plural	
I read	**čtu**	we read	**čteme**
you read	**čteš**	you read	**čtete**
he reads she reads it reads	**čte**	they read	**čtou**

Exercise 7.1

Fill in the gaps in the following sentences with the correct form of **číst** *(the correct form is indicated by the pronoun in brackets).*

1   Co (vy) .... ?

2   (Já) ne .... to.

3   Kdo to .... ?

4   (Oni) ne .... tu knihu.

5   Často (my) ....

6   (Ty) ne .... ?

Other verbs which follow this pattern include:

chtít	to want
krást	to steal
mýt	to wash; to wash up
nést	to carry; to bring; to wear
pít	to drink (stem = **pij**)
plést	to knit; to make mistakes
růst	to grow
vést	to conduct (a business); to direct; to lead; to run (a business)
žít	to live

7.2 Verbs of motion: *jít* and *jet*

The verbs **jít** and **jet** both express motion (i.e. "to go"), but **jít** means to go on foot and **jet** means to go by a mechanized form of transport (which includes a bicycle). You can easily remember the difference by thinking of **jet**-aeroplane! Both verbs follow the **číst** pattern, but are irregular in that they include a **d** in their stems. They are conjugated for you in the tables below.

First, **jít:**

Singular		Plural	
I go (on foot)	**jdu**	we go (on foot)	**jdeme**
you go (on foot)	**jdeš**	you go (on foot)	**jdete**
he goes (on foot) she goes (on foot) it goes (on foot)	**jde**	they go (on foot)	**jdou**

Now, **jet:**

Singular		Plural	
I go (by car etc.)	**jedu**	we go (by car etc.)	**jedeme**
you go (by car etc.)	**jedeš**	you go (by car etc.)	**jedete**
he goes (by car etc.) she goes (by car etc.) it goes (by car etc.)	**jede**	they go (by car etc.)	**jedou**

As you will realize, the only difference is that **jet** includes an **e** after the **j** which **jít** does not. They are, however, two distinct verbs, **jít** being used for all of "to go", "to come" and "to walk" and **jet** for "to travel", or "to ride" in some form of mechanized transport. Note, though, that "to drive" (i.e. <u>you</u> are doing the driving yourself, rather than having a lift in someone else's vehicle) is **řídit** (third conjugation) and "to fly" in an aeroplane is **létat** (first conjugation).

Exercise 7.2

*Translate the following sentences into Czech, using **jít** or **jet** as appropriate. (The words in brackets indicate only which verb is required – you are not expected to translate them.)*

1   He is going there (by bus).

2   They are walking.

3   I am going (on foot).

4   He is walking.

5   We are not going there (by train).

6   You (singular) are not walking.

7   Are they going (on foot) or going (by bus)?

8   She is not walking; she is going (by tram).

9   You (plural) are going (by train).

10 He is not going (by bicycle).

That's all the new material we're going to cover in this chapter. Now that we've looked at the four conjugations and introduced some of the more important irregular verbs, it's time for you to prove to yourself how much you've learned. The dialogue which follows uses material from all the previous chapters and is, we think you'll agree, quite a realisti con-versation – very far from the simple, and slightly artificial, sentences you were translating only a few chapters ago. As with all the dialogues, take it in stages.

1   Read it through quite quickly to get the gist of it.

2   Go through it in more detail, making sure that you understand not only every word, but also why the words take the endings they do.

3   If there's anything of which you're uncertain, don't leave it thinking, "well, I sort of understand the meaning" –

pretend that it's someone else who doesn't understand, and go through the earlier chapters until you're sure that you can explain it to them. Best of all, write the explanation down using as simple terminology as you can.

4   Write out a translation before looking at ours.

5   Look at your translation. The English may seem a bit stilted. If it does, replace it with words that we would actually use in everyday English speech.

6   Compare your translation with ours.

7   If you made any mistakes, look back through the previous chapters, make certain that you understand exactly what your mistake involved, and write yourself out an explanation designed to ensure that you wouldn't make the same mistake again.

Vocabulary

cesta (*f*)	way; road; journey; trip
často	often; frequently
dolů	down; downstairs
drahý	dear; expensive
firma (*f*)	firm
jednoduchý	simple
nahoru	up; upstairs
naproti	opposite
nějaký	some; something
obyčejný	ordinary; common; usual
odpoledne (*n*)	afternoon
potrava (*f*)	food
potraviny (*pl*)	groceries
rohlík (*m*)	(bread) roll
samozřejmě	of course
stejný	the same; identical; equal
teplý	warm
unavený	tired
"U zvonu"	"At the Bell" (name of building used as an art gallery)

výstava (f)	exhibition
že (*conjunction*)	that
život (m)	life

7.3 Dialogue

DIALOGUE

A: Ahoj. Kam jdeš?

B: Ahoj. Jdu do obchodního domu. Potřebuji koupit čaj, kávu, chléb, nějaké rohlíky, samozřejmě (!) pivo – a taky mám doma málo cukru. A kam jdeš ty?

A: Jdu taky tam. Máme stejnou cestu. Ale nejdu pro jídlo. Potřebuji teplý svetr.

B: Tamhle naproti je obchod, kde prodávají svetry a velmi krásné.

A: Ano, krásné, ale taky drahé – chci je nějaký obyčejný.

B: Co děláš odpoledne? V domě "U zvonu" je zajímavá výstava.

A: Vím, že je velmi zajímavá, ale dnes tam nejdu. Jsem unavený.

B: A co dělá tvá rodina? Jak se všichni mají.

A: Manželka má novou práci u jedné zahraniční firmy. Dcera už chodí do školy. A co tvá sestra? Je ještě svobodná?

B: Ne, je vdaná, ale bratr je rozvedený.

A: Život není jednoduchý! A ty máš jednoho syna?

B: Ano, ten už je velký. Studuje; chce být lékař.

A: To je těžké.

B: Tak tady je obchodni dům. Já jdu dolů. Tam jsou potraviny. Ty nahoru. Ahoj.

A: Ahoj.

TRANSLATION

A: Hullo. Where are you going?

B: Hi. I'm going to the department store. I need to buy tea, coffee, bread, some rolls, beer – of course! – and I've got little (i.e. not much) sugar at home. And where are you off to?

A: I'm going there too. We're going the same way. But I'm not going for food. I need a warm sweater.

B: There's a shop opposite the department store where they sell sweaters – and very beautiful (they are too).

A: Yes, beautiful, but pricey as well. I just want something ordinary.

B: What are you doing in the afternoon? There's an interesting exhibition in the house "At the Bell".

A: I know. It's interesting, but I'm not going there today. I'm tired.

B: And what's your family up to? How is everybody?

A: My wife's got a new job with a foreign firm. My daughter's at (goes to) school. And (anyway) what about your sister? Is she still unmarried (single)?

B: No, she's married, but my brother's divorced.

A: Life isn't simple! And you've got one son?

B: Yes, he's grown up (big). He's studying; he wants to be a doctor.

A: That's difficult.

B: Here's the department store. I'm going downstairs. The foods are there. You('re going) up. Cheerio.

A: 'Bye now.

Chapter 8

- Nouns and adjectives in the nominative plural,
  including special rules for masculine animates
- Pronouns in the nominative plural
- Nouns, adjectives and pronouns in the accusative plural

8.1 Nouns: nominative plural

So far, we have used only singular forms of nouns. In this
lesson we shall look at their plural forms in the nominative
and accusative cases and, in Lesson 9, we shall cover the
genitive plural. By now, you will be familiar with the idea of
changing endings: all we are doing here is filling in another
part of the puzzle which is a foreign language. The table
below shows the singular and plural forms of nouns in the
nominative case. As usual, compare what is new with what
you already know.

	Hard		Soft	
Gender	Singular	Plural	Singular	Plural
Masc. animate	student	studenti	muž	muži
Masc. inanimate	most	mosty	pokoj	pokoje
Fem. ("a" or "e" ending)	žena	ženy	židle	židle
(consonant ending)	místnost	místnosti	skříň	skříně
Neuter	město	města	moře	moře
("i" or "e" ending)	náměstí	náměstí	děvče	děvčata

Exercise 8.1

In the vocabulary below, all of the nouns are in the singular. Practise what you have learned above by putting them into the plural.

In Prague	*use:* **V Praze**
there are	*use:* **jsou**
shop	**obchod** (*m*)
church	**kostel** (*m*)
palace	**palác** (*m*)
live	**žít** (conjugate as **pít** – see paragraph 7.1)
foreigner	**cizinec** (*m*)
cat	**kočka** (*f*)
It's Christmas	**jsou vánoce** (in Czech, "Christmas" is a plural noun)
delicacy	**lahůdka** (*f*)
turkey-hen	**krůta** (*f*)
turkey	**krocan** (*m*)
goose	**husa** (*f*)
furniture	**nábytek** (*m*)
occasional table	**stolek** (*m*)
armchair	**křeslo** (*n*)

1 In Prague there are theatres, cinemas, bridges, streets, shops, squares, churches, and palaces.

2 In Prague live men, women, girls, students, foreigners, and cats.

3 It's Christmas. In the shops are bottles of wine, delicacies, turkey-hens, turkeys, and geese.

4 Here they sell furniture. Here there are cupboards, chairs, beds, tables, armchairs, and pictures too.

8.2 Masculine animate nouns: pronunciation note

Although nouns whose singular ends in **-d**, **-t**, and **-n** (such as student, kamarád, pán) are hard nouns, when they have an **-i** ending – as they do here – these hard consonants are pronounced <u>softly</u> as if they were **-d'**, **-t'** and **-ň**.

8.3 Masculine animate nouns: four consonant changes

If the singular form of the noun ends in **-h**, or **-ch**, or **-k**, or **r**, then these consonants change as follows before adding their **i** ending for the plural:

-h	becomes	**-zi**
-ch	becomes	**-ši**
-k	becomes	**-ci**
-r	becomes	**-ři**

As you will realize, this has the effect of softening the consonant, and so is closely related to the rule in paragraph 8.2. To make sure that you've got the hang of this, now do exercise 8.2.

Exercise 8.2

Study the new vocabulary, then provide the nominative plural forms of the masculine inanimate nouns in the following sentences.

boy	**kluk** *(m)*
It's Easter	**jsou velikonoce** (in Czech, "Easter" is a plural noun)
carp	**kapři** *(m)*
trout	**pstruh** *(m)*
to play	**hrát** (N.B. conjugates as **studovat** – i.e. **hraji** etc.)
soccer	**fotbal** *(m)*

1   In Prague live Czechs [use the form for male persons], boys, doctors, and officials.

2   It's Easter. In the shops are carp and trout.

3   Don't you know the boys? They are brothers.

4   Who is playing soccer? The boys are playing.

8.4 Special rules for masculine animate nouns

The **-i** ending shown in the table is the most common ending for the nominative plural of the masculine animate nouns but there are two other possible endings:

(a) **-ové** which is particularly common with short words such as **syn** (son); "sons" is **synové**

and, less common:

(b) **-é** as in **učitel** (teacher), for example, which becomes **učitelé** (teachers) but note the irregular **přítel** (friend), which becomes přátelé (friends)

With some words, either ending is a possibility: for example, "gentlemen" may be either **páni** or **pánové**.

These are fiddly and complex rules, but they fall into the category of those which you should bear in mind rather than agonize over. While it's natural for you to want your Czech to be as accurate as possible, you should try to be realistic about what is practical for you to know and remember at any given stage. At this particular stage, you are concerned with making yourself understood, not with speaking like a native. If you remember the "**i**" ending as your base rule, you probably will be understood; for the rest, listen carefully to what you hear, copy it when you can, ask native speakers if you've said things correctly – and it will come in time. Don't get bogged down in exceptions at the expense of progressing through the course to learn the broad basic rules. And after that little pep talk, we'll have a look at adjectives!

8.5 Adjectives: nominative case

You already know that adjectives must agree with the nouns they're describing in .... and in .... They must also agree in <u>number</u>. The following table is a comparison between the nominative singular and the nominative plural forms. This time, though, we are going to use **nový** as our model for the hard adjectives for reasons which will shortly become clear.

Gender	Hard		Soft	
	Singular	Plural	Singular	Plural
Masc. animate	nový	nov**í**	moderní	moderní
Masc. inanimate	nový	nov**é**	moderní	moderní
Feminine	nová	nov**é**	moderní	moderní
Neuter	nové	nov**á**	moderní	moderní

8.6 Masculine animate adjectives: four consonant changes

The four consonant changes described in paragraph 8.3 for the nominative plural of masculine animate nouns apply also to adjectives plus the final i becomes í. This should explain why we used **nový** instead of **velký** as the model in the table.

Exercise 8.3

Apply the consonant changes to the following singular forms of the adjectives to produce the plural forms.

1   strohý (severe)

2   tichý (quiet, silent)

3   velký (tall, large)

4   dobrý (good)

8.7 Two further rules for masculine animate adjectives

Adjectives ending in **-ský** and **-cký** become **-ští** and **-čtí** respectively. So:

Český muž (the Czech man)
    but   Čeští muži (the Czech men)

Sympatický syn (the pleasant son)
    but   Sympatičtí synové (the pleasant sons)

Exercise 8.4

In the following sentences, put the words in brackets into the plural.

1 Tady jsou (český student).

2 To jsou (sympatický přítel).

3 To jsou (velký kapr).

4 Přijedou (anglický sportovec).

5 To jsou (strohý učitel).

Exercise 8.5

In this exercise, you have to put the following sentences into the plural. This time, we have not bracketed the words.

1 To je starý stůl.

2 To je český student.

3 Ten obchodní dům je velký.

4 To okno je velké.

5 To je sympatický chlapec.

6 Tam je teplé moře.

7 To je velký a čerstvý pstruh.

8 To už není malý hoch, to je velký hoch.

9 To je dobrý doktor.

10 To je zajímavá kniha.

8.8 Possessive pronouns: nominative plural

The following table shows the possessive pronouns in the nominative plural compared with the nominative singular.

	Masculine (second form is masculine inanimate)		Feminine		Neuter	
	Sing.	Plural	Sing.	Plural	Sing.	Plural
my	můj	**mí/mé**	má	**mé**	mé	**má**
your	tvůj	**tví/tvé**	tvá	**tvé**	tvé	**tvá**
his and its	jeho	jeho	jeho	jeho	jeho	jeho
her	její	její	její	její	její	její
our	náš	**naši/naše**	naše	naše	naše	naše
your	váš	**vaši/vaše**	vaše	vaše	vaše	vaše
their	jejich	jejich	jejich	jejich	jejich	jejich
reflexive	svůj	**sví/své**	svá	**své**	své	**svá**

8.9 Demonstrative pronouns: nominative plural

Here again, the comparison is between the singular and plural forms of the nominative case.

Gender	Singular	Plural
Masculine animate	ten	**ti**
Masculine inanimate	ten	**ty**
Feminine	ta	**ty**
Neuter	to	**ta**

8.10 Nouns: accusative plural

The following table shows the singular and plural forms of nouns in the accusative case.

Gender	Hard		Soft	
	Singular	Plural	Singular	Plural
Masc. animate	studenta	studenty	muže	muž**e**
Masc. inanimate	most	mosty	pokoj	pokoj**e**
Fem. ("a" or "e" ending)	ženu	ženy	židli	židl**e**
(consonant ending)	místnost	místnosti	skříň	skřín**ě**
Neuter	město	města	moře	moře
("i" or "e" ending)	náměstí	náměstí	děvče	děv**čata**

Now you should draw up a table showing a comparison of the nominative and accusative plurals. How many differences do you see between them?

8.11 Adjectives: accusative plural

The following table compares the singular and plural forms of adjectives in the accusative case.

Gender	Hard		Soft	
	Singular	Plural	Singular	Plural
Masc. animate	nového	nov**é**	moderního	moderní
Masc. inanimate	nový	nov**é**	moderní	moderní
Feminine	novou	nov**é**	moderní	moderní
Neuter	nové	nov**á**	moderní	moderní

Now do the same as you did for the nouns, and compare the forms of the nominative and accusative plural.

Notice that there are no special rules for masculine animates in the accusative.

Exercise 8.6

In the following sentences, put the words in brackets into the plural. (You will notice that the words in brackets are the same as in Exercise 8.4 but that, as they form the direct object of the sentence rather than the subject, they must take the accusative case.)

1 Vidíme (český student).

2 Máme (sympatický přítel).

3 Mají (velký kapr).

4 Uvidíme (anglický sportovec).

5 Máme (strohý učitel).

8.12 Possessive pronouns: accusative plural

The following table shows the possessive pronouns in the accusative plural compared with the accusative singular.

	Masculine (second form is masculine inanimate)		Feminine		Neuter	
	Sing.	Plural	Sing.	Plural	Sing.	Plural
my	mého/můj	**mé**	moji/mou	**mé**	moje	**má**
your	tvého/tvůj	**tvé**	tvoji/tvou	**tvé**	tvoje	**tvá**
his and its	jeho	jeho	jeho	jeho	jeho	jeho
her	její	její	její	její	její	**její**
our	našeho	naše	naši	naše	naše	naše
your	vašeho	vaše	vaši	vaše	vaše	vaše
their	jejich	jejich	jejich	jejich	jejich	jejich
reflexive	svého/svůj	sv**é**	svou	sv**é**	své	sv**á**

8.13 Demonstrative pronouns: accusative plural

Here again, the comparison is between the singular and plural forms of the accusative case.

Gender	Singular	Plural
Masculine animate	toho	**ty**
Masculine inanimate	ten	**ty**
Feminine	tu	**ty**
Neuter	to	**ta**

Vocabulary

bouchne	slams (third person singular of **bouchnout**)
do	into
hoch (*m*)	boy; boyfriend
hrnec (*m*)	pot; saucepan (plural: **hrnce)**
chlapec (*m*)	boy
koupelna (*f*)	bathroom
krok (*m*)	(foot)step
kuchyň (*f*)	kitchen (also "cooking" in the sense of "cuisine")
ložnice (*f*)	bedroom
mínit	to mean
nikdy	never
obývací pokoje (*m*)	living-rooms
odcházejí	going away (third person plural of **odjet**)
páni; pane	lord! (expletive)
pauza (*f*)	pause
perfektní	perfect
pitomý	stupid
pojd'te dál	come in
pořadný	proper; substantial; sound
proto	that is why; therefore
předsíň (*f*)	hall; lobby
říkáte ...	are you saying ...

sportovec (*m*)	sportsman ("sportswoman" is **sportovkyně**)
stěna (*f*)	wall; side
strom (*m*)	tree
světlý	light; bright
šedý	grey
špinavý	dirty
takový	such
tma (*f*)	dark; darkness
tmavý	dark
výhled (*m*)	view
záclona (*f*)	curtain
zákazník (*m*)	customer
zelený	green
žadný	no; none (in the dialogue: "any")

8.14 Dialogue

DIALOGUE

A: Tady jsme, pane Řeřicho. Krásný nový byt.

B: Není moc velký.

A: Tohle je jen předsíň. Pojďte dál, má velké pokoje.

B: Tenhle pokoj má špinavé stěny.

A: Špinavé? Naše firma nikdy neprodává špinavé byty. To je šedá barva.

B: A co ta malá okna?

A: Ale ten výhled! Vidíte ty pěkné zelené stromy?

B: Já je vidím. Tak proto je tu taková tma.

A: Pojďte do ložnice. Je velmi světlá.

B: Ale tady nejsou žadné pořádné záclony!

A: Tak chcete světlé pokoje nebo tmavé pokoje?

B: Chci světlé obývací pokoje a tmavé ložnice.

A: Pane!

B: Cože?

A: Míním "Naši zákazníci jsou naši páni".

B: Kde je kuchyň?

A: Tamhle.

B: Nevidím žádné hrnce.

A: Vy nemáte své?

B: Co tohle je za byt, prosím vás.

A: Naše byty jsou perfektní!

B: Tak kde jsou koupelny?

A: Koupelny? Tady je jenom jedna koupelna.

B: Říkáte, že tu máte dvě ložnice a jenom jednu koupelnu?

A: Naše byty mají jednu koupelnu, ale jsou velmi moderní.

B: Já nechci vidět vaši pitomou koupelnu. Jdu.

(Bouchne dveřmi. Slyšíme jeho kroky jak odcházejí.)

A: Miluji své zákazníky!

TRANSLATION

A: Here we are, Mr Řeřicha. A beautiful new apartment.

B: It's not very big.

A: This is just the hall! Come in, it has big rooms.

B: This room has dirty walls.

A: Dirty? Our firm never sells dirty apartments. It's grey paint. And what about the little windows?

A: But the view! Do you see those lovely green trees?

B: I see them. So that's why it's so dark in here. Come into the bedroom. It's very light.

B: But there are no proper curtains.

A: So do you want light rooms or dark rooms?

B: I want light living-rooms and dark bedrooms.

A: Lord!

B: What's that? (What did you say?)

A: I mean, "Our customers are our lords."

B: Where is the kitchen?

A: Over there.

B: I don't see any saucepans.

A: Don't you have your own?

B: What kind of apartment is this, please?

A: Our apartments are perfect!

B: So where are the bathrooms?

A: Bathrooms? There is only one bathroom here.

B: Are you saying that you have two bedrooms and only one bathroom?

A: Our apartments have one bathroom (each) but they are very modern.

B: I don't want to see your stupid bathroom. I'm going.

   (He slams the doors. We hear B's footsteps going away.)

A: I love my customers!

Chapter 9

- *Verbs: the past tense and word order*
- *Negation*
- *Nouns, adjectives and pronouns: the genitive plural*
- *Quantities*
- *Ordinal numbers and dates*

9.1 Verbs: the past tense

In English, there are a number of ways in which to say that something happened in the past: I <u>was doing</u>, I <u>did</u>, I <u>have been doing</u>. In Czech, there is only one way to express past action. We shall use **dělat** at our model.

First, you must find the **-l participle**. This is done by removing the **-t** from the infinitive and substituting **-l**. In the case of **dělat**, this produces **dělal**. This is the basic form of the participle.

Second, you must add the appropriate ending to **dělal** according to the <u>number</u> and <u>gender</u> of the subject of the sentence, i.e. the person or thing which was carrying out the action of the verb. These endings are shown below.

Gender	Singular	Plural
Masculine animate	dělal	dělal**i**
Masculine inanimate	dělal	dělal**y**
Feminine	dělal**a**	dělal**y**
Neuter	dělal**o**	dělal**a**

Third, if the subject of the sentence is in the first or second person, you add the present tense of **být**: i.e. **jsem** (singular) or **jsme** (plural) for the first person; **jsi** (singular) or **jste** (plural) for the second person. **Být** is not added in the third person. Let's work through some examples.

"She was doing":
(a) infinitive of the verb "to do" is **dělat**: remove the **t** and replace with **l** to form the participle – hence, **dělal**
(b) add the appropriate ending to agree in number and gender with the subject of the sentence: number is singular; gender is, of course, feminine; referring to the table above, the ending for the feminine singular is **-a** which gives us **dělala**
(c) consider whether the present tense of **být** is required – no: the subject is in the third person.

Thus: **(ona) dělala**.

"We were doing":
(a) infinitive of the verb "to do" is **dělat**: remove the **t** and replace with **l** to form the participle – hence, **dělal**
(b) add the appropriate ending to agree in number and gender with the subject of the sentence: number is plural; gender is unknown and may be mixed, in which case we use the masculine form; referring to the table above, the ending for the masculine plural is **-i** which gives us **dělali**
(c) consider whether present tense of **být** is required – yes: the subject is in the first person plural – so we add **jsme**.

Thus: **(my) jsme dělali**.

Now imagine that you are asking a man, whom you have known for several years, what he's been doing.
(a) infinitive of the verb "to do" is **dělat**: remove the **t** and replace with **l** to form the participle – hence, **dělal**
(b) add the appropriate ending to agree in number and gender with the subject of the sentence: number is singular and, because it's a man and you have known him for some time, you may use the singular form of the second person; gender is, of course, masculine and he is, we hope, animate; referring to the table above, there is no extra ending for the masculine animate singular, which leaves us with **dělal**

(c) consider whether present tense of **být** is required – yes: the subject is in the second person singular – and so we add **jsi**.

Thus: **Co jsi dělal?**

For our final example, we'll use the verb "to speak"; imagine asking a woman, who is considerably senior to you at work, if she was speaking at yesterday's conference. Try to work this out before looking at our step-by-step analysis. The steps are exactly the same as in the three examples above.

(a) infinitive of the verb "to speak" is **mluvit**: remove the **t** and replace with **l** to form the participle – hence, **mluvil**
(b) add the appropriate ending to agree in number and gender with the subject of the sentence: number is singular (because you are not on familiar terms with this woman, you must use the plural form of the second person but it is the **být** element which takes the plural form, not the participle); gender is, of course, feminine; referring to the table above, the ending for the feminine singular is **-a**, which gives us **mluvila**
(c) consider whether present tense of **být** is required – yes: the subject is in the second person, and we are using the plural form – so we add **jste**.

Thus: **(Vy) jste mluvila?**

9.2 Past tense: negation

Negation (i.e. saying that someone did not do something or that something did not take place) is achieved in exactly the same way as in the present tense. So, if you wanted to say, "Did you not speak?", this time to a man, you would simply say, "**Nemluvil jste?**"

9.3 Word order in the past tense

We have been putting the personal pronouns in brackets in the above sentences because Czechs often omit the personal pronouns when using the past tense. When they are used, the word order is as we have given it in our examples:

First element	Second element	Third element
Pronoun	Present tense of **být**	"-l participle"
Já	**jsem**	**mluvil**

When the pronoun is omitted, however, the word order is reversed, thus:

mluvil jsem NOT jsem mluvil.

In other words, the present tense of **být** is always the second element in the sentence. The expressions **já jsem mluvil** and **mluvil jsem** both mean "I was speaking", or "I spoke". However, the pronoun is used only when the speaker or writer wants to emphasize the fact that the person represented by the pronoun was the person carrying out the action of the verb. Most of the time, then, you would use **mluvil jsem** to say "I spoke"; you would use **já** only if you needed to stress that it was you, rather than anybody else who was speaking.

When you want to say, "I was", "you were" and so on, you will, of course, need both the -l participle <u>and</u> the present tense of **být**. Thus, "I was there" is **Byl jsem tam** (or **Já jsem tam byl**, if you want to emphasize your own presence).

Exercise 9.1

Translate the following sentences into Czech.

1   We were studying.

2   I have seen the film.

3   They were making soup.

4   You (plural) were buying a sweater.

5   She was speaking yesterday.

6   You (singular) wanted a book.

9.4 Irregular -*l* participles

Of the verbs you have met so far, the following have irregular -l participles. If you have begun to make your "Ready Reckoner" of irregularities as was suggested in paragraph 6.4, you should enter them onto it. Write them out all together anyway, because you will need them for the exercises which follow.

Infinitive	English	-l participle
být	to be	**byl**
chtít	to want	**chtěl**
číst	to read	**četl**
jíst	to eat	**jedl**
jít (completely irregular)	to go (on foot)	singular: **šel; šla; šli;** plural: **šli; šly; šla**
mít	to have	**měl**
pít	to drink	**pil**
vstát	to get up; to rise	**vstal**
vzít	to take	**vzal**
začít	to begin	**začal**

Exercise 9.2

*The first part of each of the following sentences makes a statement about today (**dnes**). Complete the second part to the effect that this was not the case yesterday (**včera**). You should use the more common form – i.e. assume that you do not wish to emphasize the pronoun. For example:*

Dnes jsem unavený, ale včera **jsem nebyl unavený**.

1   Dnes mají čas, ale včera ....

2   Dnes jím hodně, ale včera ....

3   Dnes tam jdu, ale včera ....

4   Dnes je hezký den, ale včera ....

5   Dnes studuji, ale včera ....

*In the next five sentences, the reverse is the case: something is not the case today but was the case yesterday. We have left gaps for the present tense of **být** where this is required. For example:*

Dnes se neučí, ale včera **se učila**.

6   Dnes nekupuje pivo, ale včera ho ....

7   Dnes nemám čas, ale včera .... ho ....

8   Dnes se nevrátí brzo, ale včera ....

9   Dnes nepiješ kávu, ale včera .... jí ....

10 Dnes nejdu do kina, ale včera ....

Exercise 9.3

Translate into Czech.

Yesterday I got up in the morning. It was a nice day. I wanted to go to town. In the afternoon I went to a restaurant. I had a coffee. I began to read a new book. Then I met my friend and I did not read. My friend ate vegetable salad. I was not hungry but I was thirsty. I drank juice.

Exercise 9.4

As the next paragraphs will deal with the plurals of nouns and adjectives in the genitive case, let's recap on plurals in the nominative and accusative while consolidating what we've just done on the past tense. What we'd like you to do here is to complete the following sentences by putting the words in brackets into the plural. When you've done that, translate the sentence into English.

1 Máte tady (nějaká česká kniha) ....

2 Viděli jsme tam (náš známý) ....

3 Koupili (čokoládový bonbón) ....

4 Tamhle vidím (nějaký autobus) ...., ale ne číslo 11.

5 Máme (česká kniha) ....

6 Koupili (anglické auto) ....

7 Mají (hezká fotografie) ....

8 Viděli (velké a malé město) ....

9.5 Nouns: genitive plural

The following table shows the singular and plural forms of nouns in the genitive case.

Gender	Hard Singular	Hard Plural	Soft Singular	Soft Plural
Masculine animate	studenta	studentů	muže	mužů
Masculine inanimate	mostu	mostů	pokoje	pokojů
Feminine ("a" or "e" ending)	žemy	žen	židle	židlí
(consonant ending)	místnosti	místností	skříně	skříní
Neuter	města	měst	moře	moří
("i" or "e" ending)	náměstí	náměstí	děvčete	děvčat

Now compare the nominative and accusative plurals with the genitive plurals shown above, and draw up your own table showing the plural forms of the nouns in all three cases.

9.6 Adjectives: genitive plural

This is easy!! Two rules:

(a) hard adjectives take the ending **-ých** in all genders
(b) soft adjectives take the ending **-ch** in all genders

For the sake of uniformity, here is the table comparing the singular and plural forms of adjectives in the genitive case.

Gender	Hard Singular	Hard Plural	Soft Singular	Soft Plural
Masc. animate	nového	nových	moderního	moderních
Masc. inanimate	nového	nových	moderního	moderních
Feminine	nové	nových	moderní	moderních
Neuter	nového	nových	moderního	moderních

Exercise 9.5

Complete the following sentences with the correct forms of the words in brackets.

1   Tady je mnoho (dobrá kniha) ....

2   Potřebujeme ještě asi pět (židle) ....

3   Znám už mnoho (české slovo) ....

4   Stálo to deset (koruna) .... deset (haléř) ....

5   Jsou na návštěvě u (naši rodiče) ....

6   Byli tam všichni kromě (student) ....

7   Navštívil mnoho (galerie) .... a viděl mnoho velmi (zajímavý obraz) ....

8   Neučili se a teď' se bojí (zkouška) ....

9   Vždycka měla mnoho (starost) ....

10 Zeptali jsme se (ten chlapec a dívka) ....

9.7 Possessive pronouns: genitive plural

The following table shows the possessive pronouns in the genitive plural compared with the genitive singular.

	Masculine		Feminine		Neuter	
	Singular	Plural	Singular	Plural	Singular	Plural
my	mého	**mých**	mé	**mých**	mého	**mých**
your	tvého	tv**ých**	tvé	tv**ých**	tvého	tv**ých**
his and its	jeho	jeho	jeho	jeho	jeho	jeho
her	jejího	jej**ích**	její	jej**ích**	jejího	jej**ích**
our	našeho	naš**ich**	naši	naš**ich**	našeho	naš**ich**
your	vašeho	vaš**ich**	vaši	vaš**ich**	vašeho	vaš**ich**
their	jejich	jejich	jejich	jejich	jejich	jejich
reflexive	svého	sv**ých**	své	sv**ých**	svého	sv**ých**

9.8 Demonstrative pronouns: genitive plural

We have set this out for you in tabular form for consistency, but notice that the genitive plural is the same in all genders.

Gender	Singular	Plural
Masculine	toho	**těch**
Feminine	té	**těch**
Neuter	toho	**těch**

9.9 Quantities: *kolik ...?*

In paragraph 5.4, we explained that, when we meet a word which indicates a <u>quantity</u> of something, the noun which follows must take the genitive case. **Kolik** ...? means "how much ... ?" or "how many ...?" and, like **tolik**, **hodně**, **trochu**, **málo** and **mnoho**, is followed by the genitive plural.

When a <u>specific number</u> is involved, however, the case of the following noun varies as follows.

(a) If only one person or object is involved as the subject of the sentence, then, as usual, you would use the nominative case and the nominative form of **jeden** as given in paragraph 3.9, remembering to make "one" (**jeden**) agree in gender.

If only one person or object is involved as the direct object of the sentence, then, as you would expect, you use the accusative singular form of the noun, remembering to make "one" (**jeden**) agree in gender. Thus:

I have one student.	Mám **jednoho** studenta (masc. animate).
I have one table.	Mám **jeden** stůl (masc. inanimate).
I have one chair.	Mám **jednu** židli (feminine).
I have one armchair.	Mám **jedno** křeslo (neuter).

(b) If two, three or four persons or objects are involved as the subject of the sentence, then you use the nominative forms of **dva**, **tři** or **čtyři** together with the nominative plural of the nouns concerned. Thus:

Three (male) students have just arrived.   **Tři studenti** právě přijeli.

If two, three or four persons or objects are involved as the direct object of the sentence, then, as you would expect, you use **dva**, **tři** or **čtyři** together with the accusative plural forms of the nouns. Thus:

We know two Czech students.   Známe **dva české studenty**. (masc.)

I have four Czech crowns.   Mám **čtyři koruny**. (feminine)

(c) If <u>more than four</u> persons or objects are involved, <u>no matter what part they play in the sentence</u>, then you use the <u>genitive</u> plural of the noun. Thus.

We know seven students.   Známe sedm **studentů** (masc. animate).

I have five tables.   Mám pět **stolů** (masc. inanimate).

We have fifty Czech crowns.   Máme padesát **korun** (feminine).

You can put these rules into practice in the following exercise.

Exercise 9.6

The nouns and adjectives in brackets are in the nominative singular. Using the rules you have just learned, fill in the blanks with their correct forms according to their role in the sentence, and with the numerals spelled out in words.

1   Kolik je tam (pokoj) ....? Jsou tam 4 (malý pokoj) .... ale mnoho (velký pokoj) ....

2   Kolik (velká skříň) .... je tam? Jsou tam jenom 3 ....

3   Kolik (moderní auto) .... jste tam viděli? Viděli jsme tam 4 ...., ale 1 velmi (staré auto).

4   Kolik (muž a žena) .... se zúčastnilo toho maratónu? 4 (žena), mnoho (muž).

5   Kolik (historický dům) .... stojí na náměsti?

6   Kolik (velký stůl) .... máte doma? Máme 2 ....

7   Kolik (český student) .... tady máte? Máme tady 4. (Ten český student) .... právě přicházejí.

8   Kolik (dívka) .... se zúčastnilo finále MISS? Myslím, že to bylo 12 (krásná dívka), ale jenom 3 .... vyhrály.

9   Kolik (přítel) .... jsi pozval? Pozval jsem všechny, ale jenom 4 .... nepřišli.

9.10 Ordinal numbers

Ordinal numbers are those which show the position of an item or person in relation to others. Learn the ordinals from 1st to 31st, and you'll be able to express the date. Compare them with the cardinal numbers in paragraph 3.7 and mark any points of resemblance.

1st	první
2nd	druhý
3rd	třetí
4th	čtvrtý
5th	pátý
6th	šestý
7th	sedmý
8th	osmý
9th	devátý
10th	desátý
11th	jedenáctý
12th	dvanáctý
13th	třináctý
14th	čtrnáctý
15th	patnáctý
16th	šestnáctý
17th	sedmnáctý
18th	osmnáctý
19th	devatenáctý
20th	dvacátý
21st	dvacátý první
22nd	dvacátý druhý
23rd	dvacátý třetí
24th	dvacátý čtvrtý
25th	dvacátý pátý
26th	dvacátý šestý
27th	dvacátý sedmý
28th	dvacátý osmý
29th	dvacátý devátý
30th	třicátý
31st	třicátý první

9.11 Kolikátého je dnes? (What is the date today?)

This builds usefully on your knowledge of the ordinal numbers and of the months. In paragraph 6.6, we explained that all the months except **září** are masculine inanimate nouns and, in paragraph 5.3, that they are one of the special groups of masculine inanimate nouns whose genitive ends in **-a** rather than **-u**.

If we take "the first of January" as our example, the "of" indicates that the genitive should be used, thus: **ledna**. There are three exceptions to this, as follows:

červen	červen**ce**
listopad	listopad**u**
prosinec	prosin**ce**

Contrary to what you might expect, "the first" is treated as an <u>adjective</u>. As adjectives have to agree with their nouns in number, gender and case, the form of the ordinal number that we need is the singular, masculine inanimate, genitive.

"First" is **první** – a soft adjective – and so, to say "the first of January", we say **prvního ledna**.

So what about "the fifth of October"?

(a) genitive masculine inanimate singular of "fifth" (**pátý** – a hard adjective): pát**ého**

(b) genitive singular of October: říj**na**

Exercise 9.7

Translate the following dates into Czech.

1 The fourth of November

2 The thirtieth of September

3 The twenty-fourth of June

4 The seventeenth of August

5 The sixth of November

6 The fifth of December

7 The third of January

8 The thirteenth of February

9 The second of May

10 The thirtieth of April

11 The fifth of May

12 The fourth of July

13 The seventh of October

Vocabulary

a	and
árie (*f*)	aria
bonbón (*m*)	sweet
brzo	soon; before long
čokoládový	chocolate (adjective)
dort (*m*)	cake
film (*m*)	film; movie
finále (*n*)	final (as in "cup final", for example)
galerie (*f*)	art gallery
haléř (*f*)	heller (the smaller unit of Czech currency as pence are to pounds)

hlad (*m*)	hunger (use in Exercise 9.3 for "hungry"; you will learn how to express feelings such as hunger, cold etc. in paragraph 11.12)
hospoda (*f*)	pub
lidé (*pl*)	people
kavárna (*f*)	café; coffee-house
koruna (*f*)	Crown (Czech currency)
nádherný	beautiful; wonderful; fabulous
nejdřív	first of all (literally: "earliest" – an alternative to **první** when you want to describe the first thing you did in a sequence of events)
nepřišli	they haven't come (arrived)
opera (*f*)	opera
peněženka (*f*)	purse
peníz (*m*)	coin
plný	full
po	after
počítat	to count
poezie (*f*)	poetry
polibek (*m*)	kiss
políbit	to kiss
potkat	to meet
potom	then
pozvat	to invite
právě	just; at this moment
přijet	to arrive
při světle měsíce	in the moonlight
rande (*n*)	date
romantický	romantic
salát (*m*)	salad
slovo (*n*)	word
starost (*f*)	care; anxiety; sorrow; trouble
šeptat	to whisper
šťáva (*f*)	juice
tisící	thousandth
tolik	so/this much/many (Thus: A: Kolik? B: Tolik.)
venku	outside
vyhrát	to win
žízeň (*f*)	thirst (use in Exercise 9.3 for "thirsty")
zkouška (*f*)	exam; test; rehearsal

známý (*m*)	acquaintance; friend (also, adjective: well-known)
zúčastnit se	to take part in

9.12 Dialogue

DIALOGUE

A: **Kde jsi byla včera?**

B: **Byla jsem na rande.**

A: **Na rande? Kdopak to je?**

B: **Je to můj nový přítel.**

A: **Je to tvůj první přítel?**

B: **Ne.**

A: **Druhý? Tisíci?**

B: **Nikdy jsem je nepočítala.**

A: **Tak kam jste šli?**

B: **Nejdřív jsme šli do kavárny. Já jsem jedla čokoládový dort a on šeptal poezii. Bylo to velmi romantické.**

A: **A políbil tě?**

B: **Ne. Ale potom jsme šli na operu. Slyšeli jsme mnoho krásných árií.**

A: **A potom jsi ho políbila?**

B: **Ne. A po opeře jsme šli na pivo. Hospoda byla plná lidí.**

A: **Takže tě nepolíbil?**

B: **Políbil mě. Venku při světle měsíce.**

A: **Jak nádherné!**

B: **Byl to náš první polibek.**

TRANSLATION

A: Where were you yesterday?

B: I was on a date.

A: On a date? Who is he?

B: He's my new friend (boyfriend).

A: Is he your first boyfriend?

B: No.

A: The second? The thousandth?

B: I never counted them.

A: So where did you go?

B: First we went to a café. I ate a chocolate cake and he whispered some poetry. It was very romantic.

A: And did he kiss you?

B: No. But then we went to an opera. We heard a lot of lovely arias.

A: And then did you kiss him?

B: No. And after the opera we went for a beer. The pub was full of people.

A: So he didn't kiss you?

B: He kissed me. Outside in the moonlight.

A: How beautiful!

B: It was our first kiss.

Chapter 10

- *Expressing likes and dislikes*
- *Verbs: "to know" (**vědět** and **znát**)*
- *Negative question forms*
- *Modal verbs*

10.1 Expressing likes and dislikes – *mám rád*

Think back to **jak se máte** in Lesson 2 (2.8) and to the literal translation of that phrase as "how (do) you have yourself?".

The constructions for expressing like and dislike are very similar to **jak se máte** and, here again, the literal translation seems amusingly "foreign" to people accustomed to using the verb "to like". In Czech, to say you like something, you say that you "have it gladly". So, you need:

(a) the correct person of the present tense of **mít** (to have)
(b) the word for the "gladly" part which is **rád** and which varies according to the number and gender of those doing the liking:
   rád (masc. sing.), **rádi** (masc. pl.)
   ráda (fem. sing.), **rádi** (fem. pl.)
(c) the noun which is the direct object of the sentence – i.e. the thing you like.

Let's assume that you are a woman and you want to say, "I like wine."

(a) first person singular of **mít**: **mám**
(b) the feminine singular form of **rád**: **ráda**
(c) the noun "wine" in the accusative case: **víno**.

Thus: **Mám ráda víno.**

Another example: "We like dumplings."

(a) first person plural of **mít: máme**
(b) the plural form of **rád: rádi**
(c) the noun "dumpling" in the accusative case (and in the plural): **knedlíky.**

Thus: **Máme rádi knedlíky.**

10.2 *Rád dělám*

This is the formula you use when you want to say, not that you like a particular person, thing or place, but that you like <u>doing</u> something – for example, "I like drinking coffee". For this, you need:

(a) the appropriate form of **rád**, which is exactly the same as above
(b) the correct form of the verb expressing what it is that is liked according to who is <u>doing</u> the liking
(c) the accusative form of the noun – if, indeed, there is one.

So, let's assume you are a man, and you want to say, "I like drinking coffee". You need:

(a) the correct form of **rád: rád**
(b) the first person singular of **pít: piju**
(c) the noun "coffee" in the accusative case: **kávu.**

Thus: **Rád piju kávu.**

Another example: "She does not like drinking wine". You need:

(a) the correct form of **rád: ráda** (since the subject of the sentence is feminine)
(b) the third person singular of **pít: pije**
(c) the noun "wine" in the accusative case: **víno.**

However, we are dealing here with a negative statement which means we must decide which of the two expressions (the liking or the drinking) is to take the **ne-** prefix. Whichever verb takes the **ne-** prefix goes at the beginning of the sentence. Note also that, when it is **rád** which takes the prefix, the **á** drops its accent. Thus: **Nerada pije víno** is a translation of the sentence in its English sense. If, however, we had said: **Nepije ráda víno** this means "she likes not drinking wine".

Exercise 10.1

Translate the following sentences into Czech.

1   I like to drink coffee.

2   She likes to eat dumplings.

3   We don't like being here.

4   You (*s*) like books.

5   Do they like Prague?

6   I don't like beer.

7   He doesn't like eating this meal.

10.3 The verbs *vědět* and *znát*

Both of these verbs translate into English as "to know" but there is a subtle variation in meaning between the two which can be approximated by comparing the meanings of the following sentences in English:

(a) I know where Prague is.
(b) I know Prague well.

In (a), what is known is a <u>fact</u> pure and simple; in (b), the word "know" does not express cut-and-dried knowledge but <u>acquaintanceship</u>. In the sense to "know" in (a), the Czech verb is **vědět: Vím, kde je Praha**. In (b), **znát** would be used: **Znám Prahu dobře**.

Here are another couple of examples.

(a) "I know what time it is." This knowledge is knowledge of a <u>fact</u>: **Vím, kolik je hodin.**
(b) "I know a good restaurant." This can be re-interpreted as "I am acquainted with a good restaurant", or "I am aware of a good restaurant", so: **Znám dobrou restauraci.**

Don't worry if you don't always manage to choose the correct verb when you're "on the spot" – you will still be understood.

Znát is a regular first conjugation verb (see paragraph 4.2). **Vědět** is an irregular verb, of course, and while we would hope that you would be able to find it on your "Ready Reckoner" of irregular verbs, you may remember that we conjugated it for you in paragraph 6.4.

10.4 Negative question forms

When we say in English, "Don't you know?", this tends to carry the unspoken words, "... well, you ought to" after it, but this form of putting questions is often preferred by Czech speakers in everyday conversation. It does not carry any implied criticism, but rather what we mean when we say, "You don't by any chance know ...?". Whereas we would say, "Do you know where the post office is here?", Czechs would be more likely to say, "Don't you know where the post office is here?" This, of course, means that you would have to use the negative form of **vědět**:

Nevíte, kde je tady pošta?

And, for "Do you know her telephone number?": **Neznáte její telefonní číslo?**

Exercise 10.2

Complete the following sentences with the correct forms of **vědět** *or* **znát** *as appropriate.*

1   (já) .... jeho manželku.

2   Bohužel (já) ...., kdo to psal.

3   (vy) .... prosím, kde je tady Dlouhá Ulice?

4   (my) .... jejich adresu, (my) ...., kde bydlí.

5   (on) už včera ...., kdy se vrátíte.

6   (ty) .... jeho auto? (já) .... jen, že je červené.

10.5 Modal verbs

Modal verbs are simply "helping" verbs used with another verb to change its meaning in some way. Modals help you express opinions rather than facts: they are concerned with ability, permission, possibility, certainty, necessity or obligation. They don't mean much on their own, requiring further explanation by the other verb – they then add shades of meaning to it. See how English modal verbs such as "can/could", "may/might", "must" etc. affect "eat" in the following examples:

I can eat chips (=ability); Can/May we eat chips? (=permission); You must eat some chips (=obligation); Must you eat chips? (=necessity); She may eat her chips (=possibility).

As you can see, modal verbs are an important part of any language once you have mastered verbs to use with them. You now know all four Czech conjugations, and so the Czech modals will give you the means to extend and refine your command of the language quite considerably. As in English, you have to:

(a) use the correct person of the modal verb, plus
(b) the direct object of the sentence, if any, plus
(c) the infinitive of the main verb.

As we introduce each of the Czech modal verbs we will give you a couple of examples.

10.6 *Moci/moct*, to be able (to); to be in a position (to); e.g. "I can"

Basically, this verb adds the second conjugation (**studovat**) endings onto the stem (**můž-**), but you should note the alternatives offered in the infinitive, the first person singular and third person plural. These forms are the **moct** forms and are the ones you will find most often in the spoken language (no matter how well the speakers do or don't know each other), while the ones given first tend to be used more in writing. Note that **moci** is more formal than **moct**.

Singular		Plural	
I can	**mohu/můžu**	we can	**můžeme**
you can	**můžeš**	you can	**můžete**
he, she, it can	**může**	they can	**mohou/můžou**

Now a couple of examples.

"They can return."

(a) the correct person of the modal verb: **můžou** or **mohou**, plus
(b) [there is no direct object in this sentence], plus
(c) the infinitive of the main verb: **vrátit se**.

Thus: **Můžou se vrátit**.

Note that negatives are formed by adding the **ne-** prefix to the modal verb, as in the next example.

"We cannot help you."

(a) the correct person of the modal verb: **můžeme** plus **ne-** prefix (=**nemůžeme**), plus
(b) the accusative of the personal pronoun "you": **vám**, plus
(c) the infinitive of the main verb: **pomoci/pomoct**.
(Note that **pomoci** and **pomoct** bear the same relationship to each other as **moci** and **moct**.)

Thus: **Nemůžeme vám pomoci** (or **pomoct**).

10.7 *Muset*, to have to; to be obliged to; e.g. "I must"

This is a third conjugation (**mluvit**) verb with one possible irregularity: the third person plural can be **musejí** as well as **musí**.

"I must get up early."

(a) the correct person of the modal verb: **musím**, plus
(b) [there is no direct object in this sentence], plus
(c) the infinitive of the main verb: **vstávat**.

Thus: **Musím vstávat** [plus] **brzo** (early).

Remember that most languages have more than one way of saying things: for example, if you can say, "I do not have to go there" in Czech, you can also say, "I need not go there". If you are ever stuck, try to think of another English form of what it is you want to say – are there words or structures in the alternative version which you can say in Czech? So, what about "I don't have to go there"? (We'll assume that the speakers are on foot.)

(a) the correct person of the modal verb: **musím** plus **ne-** prefix (=**nemusím**), plus
(b) the accusative case of "there": **tam**, plus
(c) the infinitive of the main verb: **jít**.

Thus: **Nemusím tam jít.**

10.8 *Smět*, to be allowed to; e.g. "I may"

This is a third conjugation (**mluvit**) verb with one irregularity. The third person plural is **smějí** (there is no option in **smět** as there was in **muset**). For example:

"You are not allowed to smoke here"/"You may not smoke here." (This sort of statement is likely to be accompanied by a formal mode of address, so we'll use the polite form of the second person.)

(a) the correct person of the modal verb: **smíte** plus **ne-** prefix (=**nesmíte**), plus
(b) the accusative case of "here": **tady**, plus
(c) the infinitive of the main verb: **kouřit**.

Thus: **Nesmíte tady kouřit**.

Note carefully that, if you wanted to say, "<u>Can</u> I smoke here?", you would still use **smět** because you are asking permission; you are not querying your own ability to light up and inhale. You would not use **moci**. It is important to be clear about the distinction between the two:

(a) **moci** is used when we are referring to <u>ability</u>
(b) **smět** is used when referring to a <u>permitted</u> action.

Mohu tady kouřit may be true in the sense that you are physically capable of taking out a cigarette and lighting it but it does not mean **Smím tady kouřit** !

10.9 *Chtít*, to want; to will

This is a second conjugation (**studovat**) verb with one irregularity: the third person plural is **chtějí**. For example:

"He wants to buy a new car."

(a) the correct person of the modal verb: **chce**, plus
(b) the accusative case of "new car": **nové auto**, plus
(c) the infinitive of the main verb: **koupit**.

Thus: **Chce koupit nové auto.**

"Do you want coffee?" (said to a friend in a café)

(a) the correct person of the modal verb: **chceš**, plus
(b) the accusative case of "coffee": **kávu**, plus
(c) [there is no other verb in this sentence].

… and the conclusion seems obvious BUT this is a good example of where a Czech speaker might well put the question in a negative form as described in paragraph 10.4 so, rather than "Chceš kávu?", you would be more likely to hear: **Nechceš kávu?**

10.10 The modal verbs *umět* and *dovést*
(to know how to, to be good at; and to know how to, to have the required knowledge)

The four modal verbs we have introduced above are sufficient for you to be able to reflect the ideas of what is possible (**moci/moct** and **smět**), necessary (**muset**) and desirable (**chtít**), but there are two others which you may well hear and so we are mentioning them briefly here so that you won't be thrown if you do. However, their differences from each other and from **moci/moct** are very subtle, so put them in the "useful-to-know-but-not-necessary-to-say" category.

Dovést is used when you want to express the idea that someone has the knowledge or skill required to be able to do something. It follows the second conjugation (**studovat**) pattern, is completely regular, and works in exactly the same way as the other modal verbs. Thus:

Dovede to udělat.	He knows how to do it.
Dovedeš udělat to jídlo?	Do you know how to make the meal?

Umět expresses an ability to do something specific, and which requires skill and practice – such as speaking Czech, driving a car or playing the flute. (It may help to distinguish the meaning of this verb and the context in which you might hear it if we tell you that the Czech word for "art" is **umění**

and that **umělec** (*m*) means "artist".) **Umět** follows the third conjugation (**mluvit**) pattern except in the third person plural which is **umějí**. It works in exactly the same way as the other modal verbs. Thus:

Umím česky.	I <u>can</u> speak Czech (as opposed to "**Mluvím** česky" which is simply "I speak Czech").
Umí tančit valčík.	He can dance the waltz.
Umíš hrát na flétnu?	Can you play the flute?

Exercise 10.3

Translate the following sentences into Czech.

1 I want to go to the cinema but I can't. I've got to study.

2 Is it possible to buy sugar here?

3 You must not say that.

4 She can speak Czech.

5 (My) daughter needs a sweater. I must buy it.

6 We can return now.

7 Ivana, do you want to go to the theatre?

8 Can I open the window?

9 They need not do it.

10 You must call the police.

Vocabulary

bohužel	unfortunately; I am sorry
brambor (*m*)	potato
bydletto	live; stay; reside
dostatto	get; obtain
hnedat	once; straight away
jídelní lístek (*m*)	menu (*literally*, "meal ticket")
jídlo (*n*)	meal
kino (*n*)	cinema
možný (*adj*)	possible
pak	then; after that; later on
policie (*f*)	police
přirodní	natural; plain
řízek (*m*)	crumbled cutlet/steak of veal or pork
špatný	bad; wrong; poor; evil
typický	typical
určitě (*adv*)	certainly; surely
vepřové (*n*)	pork
vezmu	*literally*, "I will take" (you will need to colloquialize this in the context in which you meet it in this lesson: **vezmu** is the first person singular of **vzít** which you will meet in Chapter 13)
volat	to call
vrátit	to return; give back; put back; come back
zavolat	to call
zelí (*n*)	cabbage; sauerkraut

10.11 Dialogue

And now, a dialogue which draws not only on the material from this chapter but from previous ones as well. As before, follow the guidelines in paragraph 7.2 to make sure you get the most out of it. Remember to try to make your translation into English as colloquial as you can – by doing this, you'll find it much easier to find the Czech words for what you really want to say, rather than being stuck with what a textbook thinks you ought to say!

DIALOGUE

A: Kde jsi byl včera? Volal jsem, ale nebyl jsi doma.

B: Hned z práce jsem šel do kina. Už jsi viděl ten nový český film?

A: Ještě ne. Němel jsem čas. Je to do dobrý film?

B: Určitě je zajímavý. Pak jsem měl hlad a šel jsem na večeři.

A: Nebyl jsi v té nové restauraci na náměsti?

B: Ano. Měl jsem typické české jídlo – vepřové, zelí a knedlíky. Nebylo to špatné.

A: Taky jsem tam byl! Jídlo je dobré a není tak drahé. A pivo tam mají velmi dobré.

B: Dostal jsem hlad! Tady je taky dobrá restaurace ....

[V restauraci]

A: Tady u okna je volný stůl.

B: Prosím tady je jídelní lístek.

A: Mají zeleninovou polévku a také řízek a brambory.

B: Já si vezmu přírodní řízek – a také brambory.

TRANSLATION

A: Where were you yesterday? I called (phoned) but you weren't at home.

B: I went to the cinema straight from work. Have you seen that new Czech film?

A: Not yet. I didn't have time. Is it a good film?

B: It's certainly interesting. Then I was hungry and went to have dinner.

A: Were you in that new restaurant on the square?

B: Yes. I had a typical Czech meal – pork, cabbage and dumplings. It wasn't bad.

A: I was there too! The food's good, and it's not too expensive. And the beer there is very good.

B: I've got hungry! That's a good restaurant there too, …

[In the restaurant]

A: There's a free table here at the window.

B: Here you go; here's the menu.

A: They've got vegetable soup and schnitzel and potatoes too.

B: I'll have a plain schnitzel – and potatoes as well.

Chapter 11

- *Nouns, adjectives and pronouns in the dative case, with special rules for masculine animate nouns and for feminine nouns*
- *Describing feelings*

11.1 Nouns: the dative case

Look at this sentence and underline the nouns: "The teacher gave the girl a book". Identify the subject and the direct object. Be careful: remember exactly what a direct object is (if you have forgotten, look back at paragraph 3.1). Write down the noun which is left over. Now do the same with another sentence: "He bought his girlfriend a rose".

The two nouns which you should have written down are "girl" and "girlfriend". If you got this wrong, go back and revise paragraph 3.1 very carefully.

If you got it right and you are already familiar with the idea of the dative case (perhaps from a knowledge of German) and when to use it rather than the accusative, you may go straight to paragraph 11.2 and the table showing the Czech forms of the dative. The circumstances in which Czech takes the dative are not, however, identical to the German or Latin usages and so you should not assume that you can skip any of the material which follows the table.

"Girl" and "girlfriend" are the <u>indirect objects</u> of their respective sentences. In the first sentence, the verb is "gave"; the teacher is doing the giving; what is <u>being</u> given (i.e. receiving the action of the verb) is the book (not the girl); it is being given <u>to</u> the girl – so what the sentence is really saying is "The teacher gives, to the girl, a book"; alternatively, we could make two sentences: "The teacher gives a book. S/he gives it to the girl."

In the other sentence, the verb is "bought"; a man ("He") is doing the buying and what he is buying is the rose (not the girlfriend); the rose is <u>being</u> bought, and it is being bought for the girlfriend, so what is really being said is "He buys, for his girlfriend, a rose", and the two sentences we could make are "He buys a rose. He buys it <u>for</u> his girlfriend".

"Book" and "rose" are thus the direct objects and take the accusative case; "girl" and "girlfriend" are <u>indirect objects</u> and take the <u>dative case</u>.

Another way of writing these sentences would be: "The teacher gave a book to the girl" and "The man bought a rose for his girlfriend". This is another way in which you can identify circumstances in which you would need to use the dative case. If you are not familiar with this business of direct and indirect objects, your best plan of action is to work it out in both ways until you become used to recognizing an indirect object at fifty paces. So:

(a) identify the subject of the sentence
(b) identify the direct object (remember that this could be a pronoun rather than the noun itself)
(c) look at the noun "left over" and consider whether "to" or "for" could be placed in front of it – if so, it is the indirect object and takes the dative case
(d) see if you can make two sentences as we did above, in which the first omits the "left over" noun, and the second includes it – to include it, do you need to use "to" or "for"? If you do, then you will need to use the dative case in Czech.

Because the distinction between direct and indirect object is so important, please take a few moments to do the following exercise which is all in English. We are well aware that your aim is to learn the Czech language, not English grammar, but the Czech structures, as you have already seen, depend on grammatical rules which, although they exist in English, are largely hidden in our everyday usage. By exposing this hidden English grammar, you will have a better understanding of what the Czech language is actually <u>doing</u> and thus build up a blueprint which you can apply to an infinite variety of situations.

Exercise 11.1

In each of the following sentences, pick out the subject, direct object and indirect object (not every sentence contains all three). Remember that pronouns stand in place of nouns.

1   Mary bought John a meal.

2   They gave a present to their teacher.

3   Is that letter for me?

4   We wish you a Merry Christmas.

5   The council awarded a grant to the student.

In the following sentences, pick out all the nouns and pronouns and write their cases beside them. For example:

He bought his girlfriend a rose: He (*nominative*); his (*dative*); girlfriend (*dative*); rose (*accusative*).

6   Did you donate your prize to charity?

7   He brought his daughter's book for the children.

8   The letter is being sent to us tomorrow.

9   The curator showed me the painting.

10   The film is brilliant – I told you!

11.2 Noun tables: dative case (singular)

Now that you understand when to use the dative case, here are the Czech nouns compared, as usual, with their nominative forms.

Gender	Hard Nominative	Dative	Soft Nominative	Dative
Masculine animate	student	studentovi OR studentu	muž	mužovi OR muži
Masculine inanimate	most	mostu	pokoj	pokoji
Feminine ("a" or "e" ending)	žena	ženě	židle	židli
(consonant ending)	místnost	místnosti	skříň	skříni
Neuter	město	městu	moře	moři
("i" or "e" ending)	náměstí	náměstí	děvče	děvčeti

11.3 Dative singular: masculine animate nouns

You will have noticed that two endings are given for masculine animate nouns in the dative case. The **-ovi** ending is more common but, when there is more than one masculine animate noun in the dative case, only the last one takes the **-ovi** ending. The preceding ones take **-u**. Consider Mr Novak: in the nominative, he is **pan Novák**; in the dative, he would be pan**u** Novák**ovi** – although **pan** and the proper name are both masculine animates, only the last one, "Novák", takes the **-ovi** ending.

11.4 Dative singular: feminine nouns

We have met consonant changes before (paragraph 8.3). In the dative case, it is feminine nouns to which these changes apply. If the singular form of the noun ends in **-ka**, or **-ga**, or **-ha**, or **-cha**, or **-ra**, then the consonants change before adding their dative ending:

-ka becomes **-ce**
-ga becomes **-ze**

153

-ha	becomes	-ze
-cha	becomes	-še
-ra	becomes	-ři/ře

Try this out in the next exercise.

Exercise 11.2

Provide the dative forms of the following feminine nouns.

1 dívka

2 Olga (proper name)

3 kniha

4 střecha (roof)

5 dcera

6 hora (mountain)

7 sestra

11.5 Adjectives: dative case

The following shows the dative singular forms compared to the nominative forms. Remember: if the noun is in the dative case, any adjective or adjectives qualifying the noun must also be in the dative case.

	Hard		Soft	
Gender	Nom.	Dative	Nom.	Dative
Masc. animate	velký	velkému	moderní	modernímu
Masc. inanimate	velký	velkému	moderní	modernímu
Feminine	velká	velké	moderní	moderní
Neuter	velké	velkému	moderní	modernímu

11.6 Interrogative pronouns: dative case

Nominative		Dative	
who	kdo	**komu**	whom
what	co	**čemu**	(to) what
someone	někdo	**někomu**	(to) someone
something	něco	**něčemu**	(to) something

Thus: **Někdo je tam** (Someone is there)
but: **Dávali jsme někomu dar** (We gave someone a present).

11.7 Verbs which take the dative case

Verbs whose meaning involve the transmission of something
from one person (or place or thing) <u>to</u> another are obvious
examples of when the dative case would be used. These
include:

dávat	to give	**radit**	to advise
děkovat	to thank	**říkat**	to say
nabízet	to offer	**sloužit**	to serve
odpovědět	to reply; to answer	**věnovat**	to devote; to dedicate; to bestow
odpovídat	to answer		
posílat	to send	**věřit**	to trust
přát	to wish		

But there are other verbs where Czech takes the dative,
despite the fact that we would find it difficult, if not
impossible, to put in a "to" or a "for". These include:

kupovat	to buy	**pomáhat**	to help
		pomoct	to help
líbit se	to like; to please; to appeal	**rozumět**	to understand
nosit	to carry; to wear	**škodit**	to harm
patřit	to belong	**smát se**	to laugh
podobat se	to resemble	**učit se**	to learn

11.8 Prepositions taking the dative case

Nouns following these prepositions take the dative case.

naproti   opposite
proti   opposite; facing; against; anti-
k; ke   to, in the sense of "towards"

Thus: **Jede ta tramvaj k zoo?**
      Does this tram go to (i.e. in the direction of) the zoo?
      Blížili se k Vídni.
      They were approaching (i.e. coming towards) Vienna.

(To say "I am going to school", meaning that you are not just going in the direction of the school building but intend to go inside it, you would say, **Jdu do školy.** Similarly, to ask if the tram goes <u>to</u> the zoo, rather than merely in the direction of the zoo, you would say, **Jede ta tramvaj do zoo?**)

Exercise 11.3

Complete the following sentences with the correct forms of the words given in brackets.

1 Nerozumím jen (to poslední slovo) ...., on nerozumí (ta dlouhá věta) ....

2 Pomáhají (ta stará žena) ...., musíš pomáhat (soused) ...., je také starý.

3 Věnujeme se (angličtina) ...., je to světový jazyk.

4 Patří ten kabát (ta neznámá dívka) .... nebo (Olga) ....?

5 Dávám přednost (káva) ...., ale on (čaj) ....

6 To není dobré. Škodí to (zdraví) ....

7 Kam jdete? Jdeme na návštěvu k (naše nemocná kamarádka) ....

8 Odpověděl jsem (ten muž) ....

Exercise 11.4

Complete the blanks in the following sentences with the correct form of the words given in brackets – you will need to use both the accusative and the dative cases this time.

1 Koupil jsem (přítel) .... (tato zajímavá kniha) ....

2 Pošleme (bratr) .... (tato fotografie) ....

3 Nabízejí (ta dívka) .... velmi (hezká sukně) ....

4 Nosíš (přítelkyně) .... (květiny) .... ?

5 Říkala jsi (někdo) .... (něco) .... ?

Exercise 11.5

Complete the following questions with the correct forms of the interrogative pronouns.

1 (Co) .... se divíte?

2 (Kdo) .... radíte?

3 Pomáháte (někdo) .... ?

4 Rozumíte (něco) .... ?

5 Řeknou to (někdo) .... ?

11.9 Personal pronouns: dative case

The following table shows the dative forms of the personal pronouns as compared to their nominative forms.

Singular				Plural			
Nominative		Dative		Nominative		Dative	
I	**já**	to me	**mi (mně)**	we	**my**	to us	**nám**
you	**ty**	to you	**ti (tobě)**	you	**vy**	to you	**vám**
he	**on**	to him	**mu (jemu)**		**oni**		
she	**ona**	to her	**jí**	they	**ony**	to them	**jim**
it	**ono**	to it	**mu (jemu)**		**ona**		

The longer forms are used in the same circumstances as the longer forms in other cases – in summary, when:

(a) you want to stress the pronoun, e.g. "I gave it to <u>you</u>" – i.e. to you rather than to anybody else – would be **Podal jsem je tobě** but, in "I gave you a book", the more likely construction would be **Podal jsem ti knihu**.
(b) the pronoun comes after a preposition, in which case the j changes to **n** exactly as described in paragraphs 4.8 and 5.9. Thus "I am standing opposite it" would be **Stojím naproti němu**, and "He is standing opposite them" would be **Stojí naproti nim**. If you're not sure about how we produced these sentences, revise the explanation in paragraphs 4.8 and 5.9.

Exercise 11.6

The pronouns given in brackets in the sentences below are in their nominative forms. Each of the sentences requires the pronoun to be in the dative case. Fill in the blanks (remembering to make the necessary changes when the pronoun is preceded by a preposition) and examine each example carefully to make sure you understand why the dative is necessary.

1 Jdete k (my) .... nebo k (oni) .... ?

2 Ještě nevíme, kam jedeme. Asi k (ona) ....

3 Věříme (vy) ....

4 Proti (ty) .... nic nemáme.

5 Jedeme k (on) .... a potom k (ona) ....

11.10 Possessive pronouns: dative case

	Masculine		Feminine		Neuter	
	Nom.	Dative	Nom.	Dative	Nom.	Dative
my	můj	**mému**	má	**mé**	mé	**mému**
your	tvůj	**tvému**	tvá	**tvé**	tvé	**tvému**
his and its	jeho	jeho	jeho	jeho	jeho	jeho
her	její	**jejímu**	její	její	její	**jejímu**
our	náš	**našemu**	naše	naší	naše	**našemu**
your	váš	**vašemu**	vaše	vaší	vaše	**vašemu**
their	jejich	jejich	jejich	jejich	jejich	jejich
reflexive	svůj	**svému**	svá	**své**	své	**svému**

11.11 Demonstrative pronouns: dative case

Gender	Nominative	Dative
Masculine	ten	**tomu**
Feminine	ta	**té**
Neuter	to	**tomu**

159

11.12 Describing feelings: dative case

The dative is used in constructions such as **Je mi zima** (I am cold). Literally, of course, this translates as "It is to me cold". Similar expressions include:

Je mi zle	I am sick
Je mi líto	I am sorry
Je mi dobře	I am all right
Kolik je ti roků?	How old are you? (Literally, "How many years is it to you?")
Je nám zima	We are cold
Je jim horko	They are hot

You should also note:

Mám hlad	I am hungry
Mám žízeň	I am thirsty

As you will realize, these translate literally as, "I have hunger" and "I have thirst" and therefore have logical structures similar to the phrases you learned using **mám se** in paragraph 2.8.

Exercise 11.7

As in the previous exercise, fill in the blanks with the dative form of the pronoun whose nominative form is given in brackets.

1   Už je (ona) .... dobře, ale (on) .... není dobře.

2   Je (oni) .... to líto.

3   Je (já) .... zle. Je (ty) .... také zle?

4   (Ty) .... je zle! Nevypadáš dobře!

5   Kolik je (vy) .... roku ?

Vocabulary

blížit se	to approach; get near
dar (*m*)	gift; present
jazyk (*m*)	tongue; language
kabát (*m*)	coat; jacket
květina (*f*)	flower
navštívit	to visit
nemocný	sick; ill
okolí (*n pl*)	surroundings
poslední	last; latest
prohlédnout	to examine; look around
přednost (*f*)	preference; priority
příjemný	pleasant; nice; agreeable
rok (*m*)	year
soused (*m*)	neighbour (feminine: **sousedka**)
stát	to stand
sukně (*f*)	skirt
světový	worldwide; world-famous
škodit	to do harm
věta (*f*)	sentence
vypadat	to look
výlet (*m*)	trip
zajímat	to interest
zdraví (*n*)	health

11.13 Dialogue

Finally, here is the dialogue, which you should work through in the usual manner.

DIALOGUE

A: Kde jsi byl včera? Chtěl jsem tě pozvat na výstavu a pak do kina, ale nebyl jsi doma.

B: Mí přátelé a já jsme jeli na výlet. Navštívili jsme hrad Křivoklát. Znáš jej? Byl jsi tam?

A: Ano, je to hezký a romantický hrad. Jaká byla cesta?

B: Příjemná. Jeli jsme už ráno, tak jsme měli čas prohlédnout si hrad i okolí. Potom jsme šli na oběd do restaurace.

A: Nějaká nová restaurace?

B: Ne nová, ale velmi dobrá a ne drahá. Kde jsi byl ty? Co zajímavého jsi viděl?

A: Šel jsem na výstavu moderního umění. Viš, že se o moderní umění zajímám. Pak jsem šel do kina na nový český film. Nebyl špatný.

TRANSLATION

A: Where were you yesterday? I wanted to invite you to an exhibition and to the cinema afterwards, but you weren't at home.

B: My friends and I went for a trip. We visited Křivoklát castle. Do you know it? Have you been there?

A: Yes, it's a beautiful and romantic castle. What was the journey like?

B: Pleasant. We left early in the morning, so we had time to have a good look round the castle and surroundings. Then we went to a restaurant for lunch.

A: A new restaurant?

B: Not new, but very good and not expensive. Where were you? What interesting things did you see?

A: I went to a modern art exhibition. I'm interested in modern art, you see. Then I went to the cinema to see a new Czech film. It wasn't bad.

Chapter 12

- *Verbs: perfective and imperfective aspects*
- *Future tense (I)*
- *Nouns, adjectives and pronouns in the dative plural*
- *Telling the time*

12.1 Verbs: perfective and imperfective aspects

This notion of "aspect" is not one which we tend to come across in modern everyday English; nonetheless, the concept is not totally foreign to our language, as you will see in paragraph 13.2. Apart from the verbs of motion (**jít** and **jet**), the verbs we have used so far have all been in the imperfective aspect. We are now going to look at verbs in the perfective aspect, since we need them to form the future tense. (We shall deal with the verbs of motion separately in paragraph 13.2.)

12.2 Future tense (I)

The future tense is used when the speaker is talking about something that has not yet happened at the time he or she is speaking, e.g. "We will return on Sunday"; "He will pay tomorrow".

The future tense in Czech is formed by conjugating the perfective infinitives in exactly the same way as you conjugated the imperfective ones to form the present tense.

The following table shows the perfective aspect of some of the verbs you already know in the imperfective aspect. You will notice that what makes the perfective aspect different from the imperfective in each of the verbs in the table is a prefix.

	Imperfective	Perfective
to ask; to inquire	ptát se	**ze**ptat se
to cook; to boil	vařit	**u**vařit
to do; to make	dělat	**u**dělat
to finish	končit	**s**končit
to greet	zdravit	**po**zdravit
to learn	učit se	**na**učit se
to pay	platit	**za**platit
to play	hrát	**za**hrát
to read	číst	**pře**číst
to repeat; to revise	opakovat	**z**opakovat
to see	vidět	**u**vidět
to thank	děkovat	**po**děkovat
to wait; to expect	čekat	**po**čkat*
to write	psát	**na**psat

* note how the "e" from the imperfective infinitive (č<u>e</u>kat) is omitted from the perfective.

So, to form the future tense, the steps are as follows:

(a) <u>find the perfective</u> infinitive of the verb
(b) <u>establish the conjugation</u> to which it belongs (where the perfective is formed by adding a prefix to the imperfective, as in the examples above, both aspects belong to the same conjugation but, as you will see in Chapter 13, this is not always the case with verbs which form their perfectives in other ways)
(c) <u>add the correct ending</u> according to the subject of the sentence.

Let's work through a couple of examples.

"We will wait for you." (Assume a formal relationship.)

(a) <u>find the perfective</u> infinitive of the verb "to wait": **počkat**
(b) <u>establish the conjugation</u> to which the verb belongs: the infinitive ends in **-at**, so it is a first conjugation verb

164

(c) <u>add the correct ending</u> according to the subject of the sentence: the subject of the sentence is the first person plural, so the ending is **-áme**.

Thus: **Počkáme** (na vás).

"You will read to us." (Assume a formal relationship.)

(a) <u>find the perfective</u> infinitive of the verb "to read": **přečíst**
(b) <u>establish the conjugation</u> to which the verb belongs: the infinitive ends in **-íst**, so it is, by elimination, a fourth conjugation verb
(c) <u>add the correct ending</u> according to the subject of the sentence: the subject of the sentence is the second person in its polite (plural) form, so the ending is **-tete**.

Thus: **Přečtete** (nám).

12.3 Eating and drinking in the perfective

The verbs which are to do with eating and drinking follow the same pattern but, additionally, become reflexive in the perfective:

	Imperfective	Perfective	
to drink	pít	**na**pít **se**	(**vypít**)*
to eat	jíst	**na**jíst **se**	(**sníst**)*
to have breakfast	snídat	**na**snídat **se**	
to have dinner/supper	večeřet	**na**večeřet **se**	
to have lunch	obědvat	**na**obědvat **se**	

*These words fall into the "useful-to-know-but-not-necessary-to-say" category. They mean that **all** of the food or drink in question will be consumed. Compare:
Mám žízeň. Napiju se. I am thirsty. I will drink. (i.e. drink <u>some</u> quantity)
with:
Mám žízeň. Vypiju tu sklenici vody. I am thirsty. I will drink <u>all</u> the water in the glass.

Now do Exercise 12.1 to check that you understand how the imperfective and perfective aspects relate to each other.

Exercise 12.1

1 I am reading the book; she will read it later.

2 She is having breakfast; we will drink coffee now and have lunch later.

3 He expects her on Saturday; he will wait for her at the station.

4 Mrs Novak is cooking breakfast; Jana will cook dinner.

5 He is drinking beer; he will see us later.

6 Are you writing the letter today? Yes, but I will finish it tomorrow.

12.4 Nouns: dative plural

The table below shows the singular and plural forms of nouns in the dative case.

Gender	Hard		Soft	
	Singular	Plural	Singular	Plural
Masc. animate	studentovi OR studentu	studentům	mužovi OR muži	mužům
Masc. inanimate	mostu	mostům	pokoji	pokojům
Fem. ("a" or "e" ending)	ženě	ženám	židli	židlím
(consonant ending)	místnosti	místnostem	skříni	skříním
Neuter	městu	městům	moři	mořím
("i" or "e" ending)	náměstí	náměstím	děvčeti	děvčatům

166

When you are confident that you know what to do to the singular forms of the dative to make them into plurals, compare the dative case with the nominative, accusative and genitive cases. Test your recall of the different forms of the cases, e.g.:

(a) write out the singular in one case
(b) check that you've written it out correctly
(c) choose another case, and write out the corresponding forms in the singular, then in the plural
(d) check again to make sure that you got it right.

Draw up tables constructed in the way or ways which you feel will be most useful to you – everybody differs in this respect.

12.5 Adjectives: dative plural

Easy! As easy as the genitive, in fact. Again, there are two rules:

(a) hard adjectives add **-ým** to the stem – thus nový becomes nov**ým**
(b) soft adjectives add **-m** to the stem – thus moderní becomes modern**ím**.

This applies to all the genders. As this is so simple, you could take this opportunity to test your recall of adjective endings. First, write out the singular and plural forms in the dative, and then choose one of the other three cases we've covered to compare with it. Don't refer back to your chosen case until after you have completed your table. If you got it all right, try adding one of the others. Making up games like this for yourself is one of the best ways to make these endings sink in.

12.6 Possessive pronouns: dative plural

	Masculine		Feminine		Neuter	
	Sing.	Plural	Sing.	Plural	Sing.	Plural
my	mému	**mým**	mé	**mým**	mému	**mým**
your	tvému	**tvým**	tvé	**tvým**	tvému	**tvým**
his and its	jeho	jeho	jeho	jeho	jeho	jeho
her	jejímu	**jejím**	její	jejím	jejímu	**jejím**
our	našemu	naš**im**	naší	naš**im**	našemu	naš**im**
your	vašemu	vaš**im**	vaší	vaš**im**	vašemu	vaš**im**
their	jejich	jejich	jejich	jejich	jejich	jejich
reflexive	svému	sv**ým**	své	sv**ým**	svému	sv**ým**

12.7 Demonstrative pronouns: dative plural

Gender	Singular	Plural
Masculine	tomu	**těm**
Feminine	té	**těm**
Neuter	tomu	**těm**

Just a reminder here: because the other forms of the demonstrative pronouns are always constructed from the basic ones shown above in exactly the same way irrespective of case, we (long since) stopped laying them out for you in tabular form. Don't forget them, though: it may be that a word you think you don't know is nothing more than a demonstrative pronoun with a prefix or suffix attached.

12.8 Telling the time

Kolik je hodin? What is the time? (Literally, "how many is it of hours"?)

"Hour" is **hodina**, and, as you would expect from its ending, it is feminine. What you learned in paragraph 9.9 on counting numbers applies here too: the singular is used only for "one o'clock", the accusative plural for "two, three and four o'clock" and the genitive plural for "five o'clock" onwards. To specify the hour, you will need the cardinal numbers which we looked at in paragraph 3.7.

Je jedna hodina.	It is one o'clock.
Jsou dvě hodiny.	It is two o'clock.
Jsou tři hodiny.	It is three o'clock.
Jsou čtyři hodiny.	It is four o'clock.
Je pět hodin.	It is five o'clock.
Je šest hodin.	It is six o'clock.
Je sedm hodin.	It is seven o'clock . . . and so on up to twelve.

12.9 Half past the hour

You will need to draw on two previous topics here:

(a) adjectives in the genitive case (paragraph 5.7)
(b) ordinal numbers (paragraph 9.10)

This is because the literal translation is "half of the [whatever]th hour".

There is a fundamental difference between Czech and English when talking about 4.30, 5.30 etc. (if you have studied German, you can probably guess what it is). Times such as these involve a half hour no matter which language you are using but, while this is "half past four" for us, it is "half towards five" for Czech speakers. So, both languages specify the half, but while English relates that half to the preceding hour, Czech relates it to the coming hour. A misunderstanding here could cause you to be an hour late for an appointment, so make sure you are clear on this!

Let's do an example: "It is half past four", i.e. 4.30. Czech perceives this 4.30 as "half towards five". So:

It is	**Je**
half (towards)	**půl**
(literally, the fifth [hour])	**páté.**

Do you understand how we arrived at **páté**? "Hour", a feminine noun, is implied, and "fifth" is its adjective. "Fifth" is **pátý** in the nominative and, therefore, because it is a hard adjective, is **páté** in the genitive.

Now, let's try, "It is half past two", i.e. 2.30. Czech perceives this 2.30 as "half towards three". So:

It is	**Je**
half (towards)	**půl**
three	**třetí.**

Can you explain why **třetí** takes this form?

Note, though, that "half past twelve" is irregular: we use the cardinal **jedna** here for "one", thus: **Je půl jedné.**

12.10 Quarter past and quarter to

Now that you understand the mental acrobatics involved in half hours, the quarter hours will seem quite simple. We'll work out two examples in English first.

12.15: English says "a quarter past twelve"; Czech says "a quarter towards one" (i.e. Czech is already thinking ahead to the next hour, not back to time that has gone).

3.45: English says "a quarter to four"; Czech says "three quarters towards four".

Once you are clear about this, the actual putting of it into Czech isn't difficult:

(a) the word for "quarter" is **čtvrt** in the singular and **čvrtě** in the plural
(b) you need the preposition na to express "towards"

but note:

(c) you use the cardinal numbers here, not the ordinals
(d) because you are using the preposition **na**, you must

follow it with the accusative case (in fact, this isn't a problem since, other than **jeden** and **dva**, the accusative is the same as the nominative).

So, taking another two examples:

"It is 7.15." Czech perceives this as "It is a quarter towards eight". So:

It is	**Je**
a quarter towards	**čtvrt na** (remember that **na** takes the accusative)
eight	**osm.**

"It is 11.45." Czech perceives this as "It is three quarters towards twelve". So:

It is	**Je**
three quarters towards	**tři čtvrtě na**
twelve	**dvanáct.**

12.11 Minutes past the hour

Czech expresses its hours and minutes in the same way as our Speaking Clock expresses minutes and seconds. Thus, "ten past seven" is "seven hours and ten minutes". Two examples:

"It is ten past seven":

It is	**Je**
seven (hours)	**sedm (hodin)**
and	**a**
ten minutes	**deset minut.**

"It is twenty-five past nine":

It is	**Je**
nine (hours)	**devět (hodin)**
and	**a**
twenty-five minutes	**dvacet pět minut.**

12.12 Minutes to the hour

To express "to", you need the preposition **za** (meaning, literally, "behind") which, conveniently, takes the accusative case. **Za** goes immediately <u>before</u> the number of minutes in question.

Here are a couple of examples:

"It is five to eight."

It is	**Je**
five to ∴ <u>preceded</u> by **za**)	**za pět (minut)**
eight	**osm (hodin).**

"It is twenty to ten."

It is	**Je**
twenty to ∴ <u>preceded</u> by **za**)	**za dvacet (minut)**
ten	**deset (hodin).**

12.13 Making an appointment

When you are making an appointment, you will want to say "at" whatever time you have in mind. To do this, simply replace **je** (it is) with **v** (at). Thus: "I shall expect you at four o'clock" is **Počkám na vás ve čtyři hodiny**.

Exercise 12.2

Translate into Czech.

1　We shall expect you at a quarter to two.

2　He will have lunch at one o'clock.

3　You (s) are cooking a meal for half past seven.

4　We will wait for the train at twenty past one.

5　I will finish at five to nine.

6　They will repeat the film at a quarter past eight.

Vocabulary

dárek (*m*)	present
chytrý	clever
koš (*m*)	basket
později	later
pozdravit	to greet (**pozdravuj** is the second person singular imperative form of this verb; imperatives – the giving of commands – are covered in Chapter 14; it should be translated here as "Greet . . .")
promiň	sorry
půjdeš ...	will you come ... (we shall be looking at the future tense of verbs of motion in Chapter 13)
svatba (*f*)	wedding
uplést	to weave
výročí (*n*)	anniversary

12.14 Dialogue

DIALOGUE

A: Půjdeš se mnou zítra v půl deváté večer do kina?

B: Ne, promiň. Já zítra pracuju.

A: Zítra? V neděli?

B: Musím udělat dárek pro mé rodiče. V pondělí mají výročí svatby.

A: To je od tebe hezké. Tak co pro ně uděláš?

B: Upletu jim koš pro jejich kočky.

A: To jsi chytrý!

B: Ale můžu s tebou jít do kina v úterý, hned po práci. Dávají dobrý film v pět hodin.

A: Dobře. Tak pozdravuj své rodiče. Tak ahoj!

B: Nashle!

TRANSLATION

A: Will you come with me to the cinema tomorrow at 8.30pm?

B: No, sorry. I'm working tomorrow.

A: Tomorrow? On a Sunday?

B: I have to make a present for my parents. It will be their wedding anniversary (literally: "the anniversary of their wedding") on Monday.

A: That's nice of you. So what will you make them?

B: I will weave (for them) a basket for their cats.

A: You *are* clever!

B: But I can come to the cinema with you on Tuesday, straight after work. There is going to be a good film on (literally: "they are giving a good film") at five o'clock.

A: Good. So send my regards to your parents. 'Bye!

B: See you!

Chpater 13

- *Verbs: more on the perfective and imperfective aspects*
- *Verbs of motion*
- *Adverbs*

13.1 More on the imperfective and perfective aspects

In Chapter 12, we looked at some of the verbs which make the change from imperfective to perfective by adding a prefix. We are going to look now at verbs whose perfective is formed by changing the <u>endings</u>. You know many of the verbs in the table already, so concentrate on what it is that happens to the imperfective to make it perfective. In particular, notice how the changes to the endings usually mean that the perfective aspect of the verb belongs to a different conjugation from the imperfective.

	Imperfective	Perfective
to answer	odpovídat	odpov**ědět**
to begin; to start	začínat	zač**ít**
to buy	kupovat	**koupit**
to clear up; to clean; to tidy away	uklízet	uklid**it**
to correct; to mend; to repair	opravovat	oprav**it**
to dress; to put on one's clothes	oblékat se	oblék**nout** se
to get up; to rise; to stand up	vstávat	vst**át**
to open	otvírat	otev**řít**
to pronounce; to express; to utter	vyslovovat	vyslov**it**
to return	vracet se	vr**átit** se
to say; to tell	říkat	ří**ci**/-ří**ct**
to show; to point	ukazovat	uk**ázat**
to visit	navštěvovat	navšt**ívit**

As quick revision of conjugations, go down the table and note which conjugation each verb belongs to. For example, the imperfective of "to show; to point" is **ukazovat** which is a second conjugation verb, but the perfective, **ukázat**, belongs to the first conjugation.

13.2 Revision of present and future tenses using the imperfective and perfective

We gave you a little practice in using the different aspects of verbs in Exercise 12.1. The following examples should remind you of the work you did there.

Imperfective		Perfective	
I am saying; I say	**říkám**	I will say	**řeknu**
We are reading; we read	**čteme**	We will read	**přečteme**
They are returning; they return	**vracejí se**	They will return	**vrátí se**

Exercise 13.1

In the following sentences, the verb is given in both its imperfective and perfective aspects. The correct ending has been added for you, so you can concentrate on deciding whether the sentence requires the use of the imperfective or the perfective. Circle the one which you think is correct.

1   Často [navštěvuji; navštívím] přátele.

2   Zítra na tebe taky; [počkám; čekám].

3   Kdy se dnes [vrátíš; vracíš]?

4   Musím [jíst; najíst se] často.

5   Hned to [dělám; udělám].

6   V neděli vždy [obědváme; naobědváme se] doma, ale tuto neděli [obědváme; naobědváme se] "U Golema".

7   Vždy [platím; zaplatím] já, můžeš dnes [platit; zaplatit] ty?

When you are describing something that you do on a regular basis, or repeatedly, you use the imperfective. Try this out in the following exercise.

Exercise 13.2

After each of the two phrases given below, and using the first person singular, choose the correct form of the verbs "to have lunch", "to answer", "to pay", "to clear up", "to visit", and "to play" to make complete sentences.

(a) **Každý den** ....

(b) **Zítra** ....

Exercise 13.3

Supply the following sentences with the correct forms of the verb in the brackets, choosing between the imperfective and perfective aspects.

1	(to write):	Ivan ted' ...... dopis. To cvičení ...... až večer.
2	(to have breakfast):	(já) Ne ......, ale dnes mám hlad musím ....
3	(to do): (oni)	Ne ...... to rádi, ale pro vás to ....
4	(to buy):	Jarmila ...... různé věci, jistě ...... i tuto.
5	(to read):	(já) Nemám čas ......, ale to je zajímavá kniha, tu si ....

Exercise 13.4

Translate into Czech.

1   He is paying.

2   They will read it.

3   He will answer.

4   We are returning.

5   Where will you have dinner?

6   I am drinking coffee.

7   I am hungry. I will eat the whole cake.

8   I will visit her.

9   What are you buying?

10 I am not thirsty. I will drink only a little.

13.3 Verbs of motion

These verbs obey different rules from the verbs we have covered so far. The first thing you must be clear about is that, unlike the other verbs you had learned up to the end of Chapter 11, the verbs of motion you know already (**jít** and **jet**) are <u>perfective</u> aspect verbs. Can you remember the difference between **jít** and **jet**? If you can't, look back at paragraph 7.2.

Chodit is the <u>imperfective</u> aspect of **jít**. Note the following points carefully:

(a) both aspects are used to express the <u>present</u> tense
(b) **jít** is used when the action is carried out only once – i.e. on the occasion being described
(c) **chodit** is used when the action is carried out repeatedly – i.e. on a regular or frequent basis.

An example should make this clearer.

"I am going to school", when the speaker means that "going to school" is what he or she is in the process of doing <u>now</u> – i.e. on the occasion of speaking – would be **Jdu do školy**.

"I go to school", when the person means that he or she goes to school not just today, but regularly – i.e. "I am <u>in the habit of</u> going to school" – would be **Chodím do školy**.

Jezdit is the imperfective aspect of **jet**. These verbs relate to each other in the same way as **jít** does to **chodit**. Look at the following examples.

"I am going for a trip", when "going for a trip" is what the person is doing <u>now</u> – i.e. they may be waving you a hasty goodbye as they say the words – would be **Jedu na výlet**.

"I go for trips" – i.e. I make a habit of going on trips; it is something I do often – would be **Jezdím na výlety**.

Now your next question should be: "If both aspects are used for the present tense, how do I form the future tense?"

(a) for **jít**, add the prefix **pů-** and conjugate by adding the present tense endings
(b) for **jet**, add the prefix **po-** and conjugate by adding the present tense endings

Thus: "I <u>will</u> go to school" is **Půjdu do školy**.
and   "I <u>will</u> go for a trip" is **Pojedu na výlet**.

Similarly, "He will go to school" is **Půjde do školy**.
and "They will go for trips" is **Pojedou na výlety**.

Before leaving aspect for the time being, it is worth mentioning that there are a number of instances in which the imperfective and perfective aspects of a verb bear no visible relation to each other whatsoever. One example is "to take", the imperfective of which is **brát** (first person singular=**beru**), and the perfective of which is **vzít** (first person singular =**vezmu**). Such instances are, fortunately, very rare.

13.4 Dialogue

In the last two chapters you've learned a great deal of new material. Now see whether you can apply it to the following dialogue. Remember our guidelines on dialogues in 7.2.

DIALOGUE

A: Víš, že Ivana dostala 1. června nový byt? Je to nové sídliště, ale stanici metra nemá daleko od domu.

B: Jak velký byt má? Už jsi tam byl?

A: Ano, minulou neděli. Má velký obývák, světlý, protože je tam velké okno. Pak je tam ložnice, malá kuchyň a velmi malá předsíň.

B: Má koupelnu nebo jenom sprchový kout?

A: Koupelnu. Je poměrně velká; celá růžová. Ivana tam už má pračku. Záchod je vedle.

B: Jsou už všechny pokoje zařízené?

A: Kuchyň a obývák už jsou zařízené, ale ložnice ještě ne. Má tam postel, ale velký problém je koupit skříně: musí být velké. Víš, Ivana má mnoho věcí, ale ložnice není tak velká. Musí koupit koberce. Chce jen určitou barvu. Jsem si jist, že chce nějakou zvláštní barvu. A zapomněl jsem, že nemá ledničku a mrazák.

B: Musí být šťastná, že má vlastní byt.

A: Je šťastná. Měla jen podnájem. Ale teď' má mnoho starostí jak zařídit byt, a co koupit.

B: To si myslím. Má ráda kolem sebe hezké věci.

A: Ty nemáš takové starosti jak dát velkou skříň do malého pokoje. Váš rodinný dům je dost velký.

B: To máš pravdu. Ale máme jiné starosti. Potřebujeme opravit ústřední topení. Brzy bude zima. Všechno musí být hotové. A pak ta zahrada. U domu máme velkou zahradu. Jsou tam ovocné stromy a pěstujeme zeleninu. A taky zařizujeme. Naše děti jsou už velké. Chtějí mít své vlastní pokoje, moderní nábytek. Stále je co dělat.

A: Musím spěchat. Slíbil jsem, že zařídím tolik věcí.

B: Chci se ještě zeptat. Má Ivana telefon? Půjdu ji příští týden navštívit. Chci dřív zavolat.

A: Myslím, že ne. Řekla, že možná za měsíc.

TRANSLATION

A: You know Ivana got a new flat on 1st June? It's in that new district, but the metro station isn't too far from her house.

B: How big a flat has she got? Have you been there?

A: Yes, last Sunday. She's got a large living-room [which is] light because there's a big window there. Then there's a bedroom, a small kitchen and a very small hall.

B: Has she got a bathroom or just a shower?

A: A bathroom. It's quite big; everything's coloured pink. Ivana's got a washing-machine there. The toilet is next door.

B: Are all the rooms furnished?

A: The kitchen and the living-room are (already) furnished but the bedroom isn't yet. She's got a bed there, but there's a big problem buying wardrobes: they've got to be big. You know Ivana has a lot of things, but the bedroom isn't that big. She must buy carpets. She only wants one particular colour. I'm sure she wants some special colour. And I forgot – she hasn't got a fridge and a freezer.

B: She must be pleased to have her own flat.

A: She is happy. She used only to have lodgings. But now she's got a lot of worry about how to furnish the flat and what to buy.

B: I can imagine. She likes to have nice things around her.

A: You haven't got these worries about how to get a large wardrobe into a small room. Your [family] house is big enough.

B: You're right. But we have other problems. We need to repair the central heating. Winter will be here soon. Everything must be ready. And then [there's] the garden. We have a big garden at our house. There are fruit trees and we grow vegetables. And we have to furnish as well. Our children are already grown-up. They want to have their own rooms – modern furniture. There's always something we've got to do.

A: I must hurry. I promised to arrange so many things.

B: I want to ask you a question. Is Ivana on the phone? I'll go and see her next week. I'd like to ring beforehand.

A: I don't think so. She said possibly in a month [i.e. that she'll have a phone].

13.5 Adverbs

In the following sentences, the underlined words are adverbs: He sings <u>beautifully</u>. I drove <u>quickly.</u> They <u>greatly</u> enjoyed the performance. We eat <u>well.</u> Look at them closely: while the verb describes some form of action, the adverb describes <u>the manner</u> in which that action is performed. You could say that adverbs do for verbs what adjectives do for nouns. Although many English adverbs end in -ly, there are many which do not; they look just like the corresponding adjective, as the following examples show:

In the sentence "They worked long and hard", both "long" and "hard" are adverbs since they describe the manner of working. <u>But</u> in "They worked long hours", "long" is an adjective describing the hours.

In the sentence "The child sat at a low desk", "low" is an adjective describing the desk. <u>But</u> in "The pilot flew low over the town", "low" is an adverb describing how the flying was being done.

In "He dug a deep pit", the adjective "deep" describes the noun "pit". <u>But</u> in "They dug deep into the ground", "deep" is an adverb telling you more about the action of digging.

In Czech, this similarity in function is matched by a similarity in construction, for the adverbs are formed by adding different endings onto the adjective stem. This is at once reassuring and potentially confusing: the "up" side is that the mechanics of forming adverbs are familiar to you since you are already used to taking a stem and adding endings; the "down" side is that you may feel yourself swimming in a sea of endings – take it slowly!

Consider the following sentences:

This is a beautiful house.	**To je krásný dům.**
She sings beautifully.	**Ona zpívá krásně.**

"Beautiful" in the first sentence is an adjective, describing the noun "house"; "beautifully" in the second sentence is an adverb, describing the manner in which she sang. The adjective "beautiful" in Czech is **krásný**. The adverb is **krásně**. So the rule here is that the **-ý** (or **-í** in the case of soft adjectives) is removed from the adjective stem – in this instance leaving **krásn-** – and replaced with **-ě** or **-e**. This is the most usual way of forming adverbs in Czech. Here are some more examples:

Adjective		Adverb	
čistý	(pure)	čistě	(purely)
dobrý	(good)	dobře	(good)
hlasitý	(loud)	hlasitě	(loudly)
hrdý	(proud)	hrdě	(proudly)
líný	(lazy)	líně	(lazily)
nečekaný	(unexpected)	nečekaně	(unexpectedly)
nepříjemný	(unpleasant)	nepříjemně	(unpleasantly)
pěkný	(fine; nice)	pěkně	(fine)
pilný	(diligent)	pilně	(diligently)
soukromý	(private)	soukromě	(privately)
špatný	(bad; poor)	špatně	(badly; poorly)
věrný	(faithful)	věrně	(faithfully)

Whether the adverb ending is **-e** or **-ě** is something which, for the most part, you just have to learn as you meet them, but here are two rules which you <u>can</u> apply:

(a) if the adjective stem ends in **d**, **t**, or **n**, the adverb ending is **-ě**, as in most of the examples above
(b) if the adjective stem ends in **l**, the adverb ending is **-e**, as in:

veselý	(merry)	vesele	(merrily)
rychlý	(fast)	rychle	(quickly)

13.6 Adverbs ending in "o"

Another distinct group of adverbs replaces the **-ý** of the adjective ending with **-o**. In this group, the final consonant of the stem is irrelevant. These include:

Adjective		Adverb	
blízký	(near)	blízko	(near)
častý	(frequent)	často	(frequently)
daleký	(distant; far)	daleko	(distantly)
dlouhý	(long)	dlouho	(long)
hluboký	(deep)	hluboko	(deeply)
jasný	(clear)	jasno	(clearly)
nízký	(low)	nízko	(low)
snadný	(easy)	snadno	(easily)
teplý	(warm)	teplo	(warm; warmly)
vysoký	(high)	vysoko	(highly)

13.7 Further rules for the formation of adverbs

If the adjective stem ends in **-ský** or **-cký**, the adverb ending is **y**, as in:

anglický	(English)	anglicky	(English)
český	(Czech)	česky	(Czech)

(Note that when you want to say, "I speak Czech"; "I speak English" etc., you use the adverb as given above – the name of the language is <u>describing how you are speaking</u>.)

Note also:

hezký	(pretty)	hezky	(prettily)

In some cases, consonant changes are required to convert the adjective into an adverb. Look at the following examples:

Translation	Adjective	Consonant change	Adverb
dry	suchý	-ch- becomes -š-	suše
quiet	tichý		tiše
well; good	dobrý	-r- becomes -ř-	dobře
light; easy	lehký	-k- becomes -c-	lehce
very	veliký		velice
expensive	drahý	-h- becomes -z-	draze
severe	strohý		stroze

Notice how, in each instance, the ý of the adjective ending is replaced by e for the adverb.

Exercise 13.5

Fill in the blanks with adverbs formed from the following adjectives:

hezký; jasný; český; anglický; lehký; dobrý; špatný

1   Dnes je ......, je ......, slunce svítí.

2   Rozumějí ...... už docela ....

3   Jde k lékaři. Je mu ....

4   To je tak snadné, dělá to tak ....

5   Mluvíte ...... ?

6   Cítila jsem se ......, mluvil velmi ....

Vocabulary

bolet	to hurt; ache
brzy	soon; early
celý	whole
cítit	to feel
cvičení (n)	exercise; practice; training; lesson

185

děti *(pl)*	children
dost	enough
dřív	beforehand; earlier
hlava *(f)*	head
horečka *(f)*	fever
hotový	ready
chřipka *(f)*	'flu
chvíle *(f)*	a while
i	and; as well as; both
jiný	other; another; different
každý	every; each; everybody; anyone
když	when; as; if
koberec *(m)*	carpet
kolem	round; around; about
konec *(m)*	end; conclusion; close; tip
krk *(m)*	neck
lednička *(f)*	refrigerator
lékárna *(f)*	pharmacy
lidé *(pl)*	people
měsíc *(m)*	month; moon
minulý	last
mozek *(m)*	brain
možná *(adv)*	perhaps; maybe; possibly
mrazák *(m)*	freezer
nakonec	in the end; finally; eventually
náledí	icy (on roads)
naštěstí	fortunately; luckily
nečekaný	unexpected
nehoda *(f)*	accident
obývák *(m)*	living-room
ochladit se	to become cold
opravdu	really; actually; indeed
otřes *(m)*	shock; shake
otřes mozku *(accus)*	concussion (literally: shock-brain)
ovocný	fruit (adjective)
počasí *(n)*	weather
podnájem *(m)*	rented room; lodgings
poměrně	relatively; comparatively
pračka *(f)*	washing-machine
protože	because; as; since
pršet	to rain
předpověď *(f)*	forecast; prediction

půjčit si	to borrow
řekla	she said . . .
rodinný	family (adjective, as in "family home")
ruka *(f)*	hand; arm
různý	different
růžový	pink; rosy
sebe	herself
si	indicates "to oneself" – reflexive
sídliště *(n)*	housing estate; development
slunce *(n)*	sun
smyk *(m)*	skid
sníh *(m)*	snow
spěchat	to hurry
sprchový kout *(m)*	shower cabinet
stále	always; all the time
svítit	to shine; light
těšit se	to look forward
to máš (máte) pravdu	you're right (literally: "you have the truth")
topení *(n)*	heating
určitý *(adj)*	certain; definite; specific; particular
ústřední	central
vážný	serious
vlastní	(one's) own
vždy	always; at all times
zahrada *(f)*	garden
záchod *(m)*	toilet; W.C.
zamračeno	cloudy; overcast (adjective: zamračený)
zapomenout	to forget (first person singular: zapomenu)
zařídit	furnish; arrange
zařízení *(n)*	furnishings
zařizovat	to furnish; arrange
zima *(f)*	winter; cold
zítra *(n)*	tomorrow
změna *(f)*	change; alteration
zpívat	to sing
zranit se	to be hurt; to be injured
zůstat	to stay; remain
zvláštní	special; particular; peculiar

13.8 Dialogue

DIALOGUE

A: Dnes je opravdu hezky. Není zamračeno, slunce svítí a už je docela teplo.

B: Už bylo načase. Celý minulý týden pršelo, pak se ochladilo. Nečekal jsem takovou změnu počasí.

A: To byla velká změna počasí, ale četl jsem předpověď počasí, tak to nebylo tak nečekané.

B: Možná ne pro tebe, ale pro mnoho jiných ano. Znáš Lenku?

A: Tvou sestru?

B: Ano, půjčila si auto a jela do Plzně. Když bylo to náledí, dostala smyk a měla nehodu.

A: Co se jí stalo? Něco vážného?

B: Naštěstí ne. Jenom otřes mozku – a zranila si ruku. Teď už je jí dobře.

A: To jsem rád. Má manželka je nemocná. Teď jdu do lékárny.

B: Chřipka?

A: Ano, minulý týden byla unavená, pak ji bolela hlava a nakonec v krku a měla horečku. Musela jít k lékaři. Tak zůstala do konce týdne doma. Teď už je jí dobře.

B: To dělá to počasí. Chvíli teplo, potom zima.

A: Musíme něco dělat pro zdraví. Chceme jet na hory.

B: Kam pojedete? Do Krkonoš?

A: Ne, tam jezdí mnoho lidí, ale do Orlických hor.

B: Je tam dost sněhu?

A: Myslím, že ano. Už se všichni těšíme.

TRANSLATION

A: It's really nice today. It's not overcast, the sun is shining and it's fairly warm.

B: About time too. It rained all last week, then it got cold. I didn't expect the weather to change so much.

A: It was a big change, but I read the weather forecast so it wasn't so unexpected.

B: Not for you, maybe, but for many others [i.e. other people: "others" is an adjective]. Do you know Lenka?

A: Your sister?

B: Yes, she borrowed a car and went to Plzeň. When the roads became icy, she skidded and had an accident.

A: What happened to her? Anything serious?

B: No, fortunately. Only concussion – and she injured her hand. She's all right now.

A: I'm glad to hear it. My wife is ill. I'm on my way to the pharmacy.

B: 'Flu?

A: Yes, last week she was (feeling) tired, then she had a headache and finally she had a sore throat and was feverish. She had to go to the doctor. So she stayed at home till the end of the week. She's OK now.

B: The weather's doing that [i.e. is responsible for it]. It's warm for a while, then it's cold.

A: We must do something healthy. We want to go to the mountains.

B: Where are you going to go? To Krkonoše?

A: No, a lot of people go there – but to Orlické mountains.

B: Is there enough snow there?

A: I think so. We're all looking forward to it.

Chapter 14

- *Verbs: imperatives*
- *Nouns, prepositions, adjectives, and pronouns in the locative case*
- *When were you born?*

14.1 Verbs: imperatives

As its name suggests, the imperative is used when giving orders. For example: "Give me that letter"; "Don't touch that". If you think about it, a command is always issued to somebody else, which implies a use of "you" (either singular or plural). What we are really saying is, "You give me that letter"; "Don't you touch that".

The other use of the imperative in Czech is where a suggestion is being made, not in the form of a question, such as "Shall we go now?" (where the person spoken to has a choice in the matter) but in the form of a command, such as "Let's go!" or "Let us give thanks", where no real option is being offered. Notice the difference in English between "Let's go" in the sense of "We're all going to move now" and "Let us go" in the sense of "Allow us to leave". In the second example, you wouldn't use "let's", and therefore you wouldn't use the imperative – it is a request rather than a command. The imperative is used only where the speaker is giving what is effectively an order.

So, taken all together, this means that to express the imperative we need verb forms for the second person singular and plural and for the first person plural.

The basis from which you work to do this is the <u>third person plural</u> in the present tense – thus, **studují** or **studujou**, **mluví** and **čtou** (you will see below why **dělají** has been omitted at this stage).

Next, you remove the vowel endings – thus, **studuj**, **mluv** and **čt**.

Then, you apply one of the following rules. It is important to be aware that these rules <u>cut across </u>the conjugations.

(a) When the third person plural ended in **-í** or **-ou**, as in **mluví** and **studují** or **studujou**, what remains after removal of the final vowels (**mluv** and **studuj**) is the second person singular form of the imperative. To form the first and second person plural, you add the endings **-me** and **-te** respectively. The following table illustrates.

			IMPERATIVES		
Infinitive	3rd person plural	Ending removed	2nd person singular	2nd person plural	1st person plural
mluvit	mluví	mluv	mluv	mluv**te**	mluv**me**
studovat	studují/ou	studuj	studuj	studuj**te**	studuj**me**
psát	píší/ou	piš	piš	piš**te**	piš**me**

(b) If, when you remove the final vowels from the third person plural, you find that the last two letters of what remains are both consonants (as with **čt**, for example), then you add **-i** to form the second person singular imperative. To form the first and second person plural, you add instead **-ěme** and **-ěte** respectively. The following table illustrates.

			IMPERATIVES		
Infinitive	3rd person plural	Ending removed	2nd person singular	2nd person plural	1st person plural
číst	čtou	**čt**	čti	čt**ěte**	čt**ěme**
jít	jdou	**jd**	jdi	jd**ěte**	jd**ěme**
říci	řeknou	**řekn**	řekni	řekn**ěte**	řekn**ěme**

Where the final consonant of the stem is **-l**, **-z**, or **-ř**, the endings may be **-ete** and **-eme** rather than **-ěte** and **-ěme**. Thus, in the case of **myslet**, for example:

			IMPERATIVES		
Infinitive	3rd person plural	Ending removed	2nd person singular	2nd person plural	1st person plural
myslet	myslí	mysl	mysli	mysl**ete**	mysl**eme**

And the same would apply to verbs such as **otevřít** (third person plural **otevřou**), **zavřít** (third person plural **zavřou**) and so on.

An important one for you to know is **pojít** which we met in the dialogue in Lesson 8, when the man from the agency invited his customer to "come in" – **pojd'te dál**. Notice how the **d** here acquires a háček and the **e** drops out.

			IMPERATIVES		
Infinitive	3rd person plural	Ending removed háček added	2nd person singular	2nd person plural	1st person plural
pojít	pojdou	po**jd'**	po**jd'**	po**jd'te**	po**jd'me**

(c) For verbs whose third person plural ended in **-ají**, **-ejí** or **-ějí**, the vowel before the **-j** is always **e** or **ě** in the imperative: thus, **dělej** NOT **dělaj**. The endings are then the same as those in rule (a) above, so:

			IMPERATIVES		
Infinitive	3rd person plural	Ending removed (and vowel changed if necessary)	2nd person singular	2nd person plural	1st person plural
dělat	dělají	děl**ej**	děl**ej**	děl**ejte**	děl**ejme**
dívat se	dívají se	dív**ej** se	dív**ej** se	dív**ejte** se	dív**ejme** se
rozumět	rozumějí	rozum**ěj**	rozum**ěj**	rozum**ějte**	rozum**ějme**

14.2 Irregular imperatives

It would, of course, be just <u>too</u> neat if every single verb fell fairly and squarely within one of these three rules – nothing in a language is ever as cut and dried as that, as you will no doubt have realized by now. The irregular imperatives which you are most likely to need are those from **být**. **Být** forms its imperatives from the third person plural of its <u>future</u> tense. The future tense of **být** is an important topic which is dealt with fully in Chapter 15, and the imperative forms are noted for you in paragraph 15.7.

Apart from that, you will realize that, for example, the third person plural of **obědvat** is **obědvají**: the **-ají** ending indicates the application of rule (c) above, but what about the two consonants you're left with after removal of the ending? (In fact, rule (c) applies to this particular verb.) It's a similar story with **pěstovat**, the third person plural of which is **pěstuji** (or **pěstujou**) thus indicating rule (a) – which is actually the one which applies – but the presence of the two consonants after removal of the ending again sets up an apparent conflict with rule (b). These are, however, exceptions which prove the rules: you will form the imperatives of most verbs correctly if you follow them. The table below lists the imperatives of some common verbs with irregularities:

			IMPERATIVES		
Infinitive	3rd person plural	Ending removed (and stem changed if necessary)	2nd person singular	2nd person plural	1st person plural
jíst	jedí	je**z**	je**z**	je**zte**	je**zme**
koupit	koupí	ku**p**	ku**p**	ku**pte**	ku**pme**
stát	stojí	st**ůj**	st**ůj**	st**ůjte**	st**ůjme**
vědět	vědí	vě**z**	vě**z**	vě**zte**	vě**zme**
vidět	vidí	vi**z**	vi**z**	vi**zte**	vi**zme**

14.3 Important note on imperatives

When the command being given is a <u>positive</u> command, for example: "Give me that book"; "Wash your hair", either the perfective or imperfective aspect of the verb can be used. However, if the command is a negative one – for example: "Don't touch that"; "Don't pull the cat's tail" – then <u>only the imperfective aspect may be used</u>.

Now try the exercises.

Exercise 14.1

In the following dialogue, fill in the correct form of the imperative for the verbs given in brackets.

NA ULICI

A: Promiňte prosím vás, kde je tady pošta?

B: (Jít) .... rovně touto ulicí, ale ne(jít) .... až na konec.

A: Děkuji, ale můžete mi říci, jak se dostanu k muzeu?

B: (Jet) .... tramvají číslo 18, zastávka je blízko pošty, ale ne(jet) .... tramvají číslo 9.

A: Mockrát děkuju.

B: Není zač.

Now translate the dialogue into English.

Exercise 14.2

Now do the same with this dialogue.

V KUCHYNI

A: Co tady děláš?

B: Ale chci něco připravit k večeři a nevím co.

A: Tak (dělat) .... ten recept, co říkala Jana, ale ne(dělat) .... toho moc, nemáme ani hlad.

B: Je to dobré?

A: Hm, (přidat) .... ještě pepř, ale už ne(přidat) .... sůl. To není zdravé.

C: Můžu si také vzít?

B: (Vzít) .... si, ale ne(vzít) .... si moc.

C: Je to výborné!

14.4 Nouns: the locative case

As its name suggests, this case is used when the location of the noun is important. If you can remember as far back as paragraph 4.7, you will recall that the words we use to pinpoint the location of something – in that case, the position (or location) of a letter in relation to a chest of drawers – are prepositions. Because of this, the locative case is sometimes referred to as the "prepositional case".

The first thing to remember, then, is that the locative case is used only with an accompanying preposition. The prepositions which can accompany the locative case are: **v** or **ve**, **na**, **o**, **po**, and **při**. To emphasize this, we have included a preposition along with the nouns in the following table. An explanation of the meanings of these prepositions when used with the locative case follows in paragraph 14.6. For now, just learn the ending changes for the locative singular as you have done for all the other cases.

14.5 Noun tables: the locative case (singular)

In the following table, the locative singular is, as usual, shown in comparison with the nominative singular. Notice too, how similar the locative singular is to the dative singular (see paragraph 11.2).

Gender	Hard Nom.	Locative	Soft Nom.	Locative
Masc. animate	student	o student**ovi** OR o student**u**	muž	o mu**žovi** OR o mu**ži**
Masc.inanimate	most	o most**u** OR o most**ě**	pokoj	o pokoj**i**
Fem. ("a" or "e" ending)	žena	o žen**ě**	židle	o židl**i**
(consonant ending)	místnost	v místnost**i**	skříň	o skřín**i**
Neuter	město	ve měst**ě** OR o měst**u**	moře	o moř**i**
("e" or "i" ending)	náměstí	o náměstí	děvče	o děv**četi**

The explanations of the alternatives offered in the table are:

(a) Masculine animate: we have met these alternatives in the masculine animate before (see paragraph 11.3). Exactly the same applies here: the -**ovi** ending is the one which is more frequently used but, when there are a number of nouns together, as in a person's name, only the last one takes the -**ovi** ending. So, picking again on Mr. Novák (preceded by his preposition for the locative case), he would again be "panu Novák**ovi**" and, if we give him a couple of Christian names, his name in the locative case would be "pan**u** Josef**u** Kajetán**u** Novák**ovi**".

(b) Masculine inanimate and neuter: the alternative endings are included because not only are you likely to hear both, but you may use either yourself. Both are correct, and every native speaker of Czech understands them; for the purposes of everyday communication there is no practical difference between them.

14.6 Prepositions with the locative case

The meanings of the prepositions which accompany the locative case (see paragraph 14.4, above) are explained below. You will notice that you have met some of them before, so be particularly careful in noting their meanings for the purposes of the locative case.

Preposition	Meaning	Notes
v/ve	at; in; inside	used when describing a state of rest; includes expressions involving time such as "in January", "in February": (see paragraph 14.12)
na	over	again, used when describing a state of rest; contrast this usage with **na** followed by the accusative, when motion is implied
o	about; concerning	
po	on (a surface); around; about; after (an event)	the use of this preposition in the locative has a connotation of <u>movement</u>
při	near; by; (occasionally) at (an event)	

14.7 Locative singular: feminine nouns

The consonant changes here are the same as the consonant changes we met in the dative (paragraph 11.4). A quick reminder:

-ka	becomes	**-ce**
-ha	becomes	**-ze**
-cha	becomes	**-še**
-ra	becomes	**-ři/ře**

Try this out in the following exercise. We have provided a preposition for you for the locative, so all you need concentrate on is the consonant changes.

Exercise 14.3

1	studentka	o ....
2	podlaha	na ....
3	sestra	o ....
4	sprcha	ve ....
5	kniha	na ....

14.8 Adjectives: locative case

	Hard		Soft	
Gender	Nom.	Locative	Nom.	Locative
Masc. animate	velký	o velkém	moderní	moderním
Masc. inanimate	velký	o velkém	moderní	moderním
Feminine	velká	o velké	moderní	moderní
Neuter	velký	o velkém	moderní	moderním

14.9 Demonstrative pronouns in the locative case

Gender	Nominative	Locative
Masculine	toho/ten	o **tom**
Feminine	ta	o **té**
Neuter	to	o **tom**

Exercise 14.4

Answer the following questions, using each of the words given in square brackets.

1 Kde bydlíte?
   V [Praha, Brno, Bratislava, Londýn, Paříž, Berlín, Hamburk, Vídeň]

2 O kom mluvíte?
   O [Marie, Petr, ta hezká dívka, ten nový student, jeho teta, můj známý, její přítel]

3 O čem diskutujete?
   O [česká kuchyně, ten velký problém, ten těžký text, ten zajímavý televizní program, ta nečekaná zpráva, jeho chování]

4 Kde máš tu knihu?
   V/ve [taška, ten velký stůl, kabelka, knihovna, druhý pokoj, ložnice, noční stolek]

5 Kde je ta peněženka?
   Na [země, podlaha, židle, skříň, koberec]

6 Kdy se vrátí?
   Po [oběd, večeře, snídaně, představení, přednáška]

7 Kdy se to stalo?
   Při [módní přehlídka, dopolední vyučování, hodina angličtiny, jejich návštěva]

8 Kde je pan Černý?
   Je na [oběd, večeře, výstava, prohlídka]

9 Kde jsou?
   V/ve [třída, jeho byt, jejich dům]

14.10 Possessive pronouns: locative case

	Masculine		Feminine		Neuter	
	Nom.	Locative	Nom.	Locative	Nom.	Locative
my	můj	o **mém**	má	o **mé**	mé	o **mém**
your	tvůj	o **tvém**	tvá	o **tvé**	tvé	o **tvém**
his and its	jeho	o jeho	jeho	o jeho	jeho	o jeho
hers	její	o **jejím**	její	o její	její	o **jejím**
our	náš	o **našem**	naše	o **naší**	naše	o **našem**
your	váš	o **vašem**	vaše	o **vaší**	vaše	o **vašem**
their	jejich	o jejich	jejich	o jejich	jejich	o jejich
reflexive	svůj	o **svém**	svá	o **své**	své	o **svém**

14.11 Personal pronouns: locative case

The following table shows the locative forms of the personal pronouns as compared to their nominative forms.

Singular				Plural			
Nom.		Locative		Nom.		Locative	
I	**já**	about me	o **mně**	we	**my**	about us	o **nás**
you	**ty**	about you	o **tobě**	you	**vy**	about your	o **vás**
he	**on**	about him	o **něm**		**oni**		
she	**ona**	about her	o **ní**	they	**ony**	about them	o **nich**
it	**no**	about it	o **něm**		**ona**		

200

Exercise 14.5

Fill in the blanks with the locative form of the personal pronoun required in each sentence.

1 Mluvíte o tom studentovi? Ano, mluvíme o ....

2 Nemluvili jsme o (oni) ....

3 Diskutuješ o tom problému? Ano, diskutuji o ....

4 Určitě o (ty) .... nemluvili.

5 Přišli až po (ona) ...., ne po (my) ....

14.12 *Kdy jste se narodil?* (When were you born?)

The first thing to note is that the form of the question above is the one you would use when speaking to a man. If you were addressing a woman, you would say **narodila.**

Narodil is the past participle of the verb **narodit se** (to be born); the present tense of **být** is added because the subject of the sentence (you) is in the second person. (See paragraph 9.1 if you have forgotten how to construct the past tense.) To reply, "I was born...", then, you would say **Já jsem se narodil** or **Narodil jsem se ...** . Of course, you then have to specify the month and, to do this, you use the locative case preceded by the preposition **v.**

So, for a man, "I was born in February" is **Já jsem se narodil v únoru**; using the alternative word order, and speaking as a woman, "I was born in September" is **Narodila jsem se v září.**

Exercise 14.6

Say that you were born in the following months, using the correct form according to whether you are a man or a woman.

1   (June)   4   (August)

2   (December)   5   (November)

3   (April)   6   (March)

Exercise 14.7

Translate the following paragraph from Czech into English.

Praha je hlavní město České republiky. Je to krásné město, kde je mnoho historických budov. Pražský hrad je asi první místo, kam návštěvníci Prahy směřují. Jdou obvykle přes Karlův most, starý most uprostřed města, odkud máte krásný pohled na Hradčany. Když neznáte Prahu, musíte se zeptat na cestu.

Vocabulary

až	as far as
daleko	far
diskutovat	to discuss; debate
dopoledne *(n)*	morning; in the morning
drobné *(pl)*	small change
chování *(n)*	behaviour
kabelka *(f)*	handbag
lístek *(m)*	ticket
muzeum *(n)*	museum
návštěva *(f)*	visit; call; attendance
nejbližší	nearest
oranžový	orange

prohlídka *(f)*	sight-seeing; visit; inspection
procházka *(f)*	walk
přednáška *(f)*	lecture
představení *(n)*	performance; introduction
přehlídka *(f)*	parade; show; display
přijíždí	is arriving (by some form of mechanized transport)
připravit	to prepare; get ready
přišli	they arrived (on foot) (**šel**, if you remember, is the "-l participle" of **jít**; we shall cover the prefix **při-** in Chapter 16)
recept *(m)*	recipe; prescription
říkala	she said
rovný	straight
snídaně *(f)*	breakfast
stolek *(m)*	small table
strana *(f)*	side (of a street)
to nevadí	it doesn't matter
touto	this
tramvaj *(f)*	tram
třída *(f)*	avenue; class; form
vchod *(m)*	entrance
výborný	excellent
vyměnit	to change (money)
vyučováni *(n)*	teaching [i.e. classes; lessons]
zastávka *(f)*	stop
země *(f)*	country; land; soil; ground; earth
zpráva *(f)*	news; report
žlutý	yellow

14.13 Dialogues

And, finally, three dialogues.

DIALOGUE 1

A: Promiňte, prosím vás, jak se dostanu na Malostranské náměstí?
B: Můžete jít přes Karlův most a potom přímo, až přijdete na Malostranské náměstí.
A: Je to daleko?
B: Ano, je to docela daleko, ale je to hezká procházka. Stojí to za to! Ale zastávka tramvaje je tamhle. Tramvaj 22 přijíždí. Je to třetí zastávka.
A: Mockrát děkuji.
B: Prosím.

DIALOGUE 2

A: Promiňte, je tady někde banka?
B: Ano, v této ulici jsou dvě banky. Obchodní banka je na levé straně a naproti je Poštovní banka.
A: To je ta žlutá vysoká budova tamhle?
B: Ano, to je Obchodní banka.
A: To je velmi blízko. Děkuji.
B: Prosím.

DIALOGUE 3

V metru

A: Promiňte, potřebuji lístky.
B: U vchodu jsou dva automaty.
A: Vidím je, ale nemám drobné.
B: To nevadí. Můžete vyměnit pětikoruny v tom oranžovém automatu a ten druhý je na lístky.
A: Mockrát děkuji.
B: Prosím.

TRANSLATION 1

A: Excuse me please, how do I get to Malostranské Square?

B: You can go across Charles Bridge and then go straight on and you come to Malostranské Square.

A: Is it far?

B: Yes, it is pretty far but it's a nice walk. It's worth it (going like that). But the tram stop is over there. Tram 22 is coming. It's the third stop.

A: Thanks a lot.

B: You're welcome.

TRANSLATION 2

A: Excuse me, is there a bank anywhere here?

B: Yes, there are two banks in this street. The Commercial Bank is on the left-hand side and opposite there's the Post Bank.

A: Is it the high yellow building over there?

B: Yes, that's the Commercial Bank.

A: It's very close. Thank you.

B: You're welcome.

TRANSLATION 3

In the metro

A: Excuse me, I need (to buy) tickets.

B: There are two slot machines at the entrance.

A: Well, I can see them, but I don't have change.

B: It doesn't matter. You can change five crown coins in that orange slot machine and the second one is for tickets.

A: Thanks a lot.

B: You're welcome.

Chapter 15

- *Nouns: vocative case*
- *Verbs: future tense (II)*
- *Summary of the system of present and future tenses*
- *Imperative of být*

15.1 Nouns: vocative case

The vocative case is used when we address someone by name or if we are trying to attract their attention. For example, "<u>Mum</u>, can you come over here a minute"; "Excuse me, <u>miss</u>"; "Thank you, <u>darling</u>"; "<u>Ladies and gentlemen</u>, I should like to welcome you to this conference"; "Shut up, <u>idiot</u>"; "<u>Waiter</u>, we would like to order now"; "<u>John</u>, look at the castle" and so on. The words which are underlined in these sentences are not essential to the grammatical structure; what they do is make clear who is being addressed. Here is a comparison of the vocative with the nominative case.

	Hard		Soft	
Gender	Nom.	Vocative	Nom.	Vocative
Masc. animate	student	studente	muž	muži
("h", "k", "ch" ending)	číšník	číšníku	—	—
Masc. inanimate	most	moste	pokoj	pokoji
Fem. ("a" or "e" ending)	žena	ženo	židle	židle
(consonant ending)	místnost	místnost	skříň	skříň
Neuter	město	město	moře	moře
("e" or "i" ending)	náměstí	—	děvče	děvče

We have maintained the same format for this table as that in all the other chapters and, if you have been following our advice as to how to go about learning the different Czech cases, you will see that very little new learning is needed for this case. As you might expect from the purpose which is served by the vocative case, the only changes of which you need take account are in the masculine animates and the feminines. (You will have noticed that there are also vocative forms of masculine inanimate nouns. These would be used only in poetic or dramatic contexts, as where the speaker addresses an inanimate object as, for example, in "Oh, bridge!", "Oh, flower!", "Oh, autumn!" and so on.) A further piece of good news is that the vocative plurals are exactly the same as the nominative plurals.

15.2 Nouns: vocative case – some examples

As we do not change the form of proper names in English, no matter how we are using the name, you might find it reassuring to have a few examples of the Czech vocative as applied to proper names and titles.

English	Czech nominative	Czech vocative
Charles	Karel	Karle
Eva	Eva	Evo
George	Jirka	Jirko
Joe	Pepík	Pepíku
Miss	slečna	slečno
Mr	pan	pane
waitress	číšnice/servírka	číšnice/servírko

Exercise 15.1

Put the names in brackets into the vocative case.

1 (slečna Nováková) ...., kde je telefon?

2 (Eva) ...., pospěš si, už nemáme čas!

3 (Jirka) ...., musíš to udělat znovu!

4 (student) ...., napište to ještě jednou!

5 (Láďa *familiar form of* **Ladislav**) ...., přijď k nám.

15.3 Verbs: the future tense (II)

In Chapter 12, you learned how to construct the future tense from perfective verbs. It is also possible to construct the future tense from imperfective verbs. Although this is slightly more convoluted, you should not have much difficulty as long as you take it slowly and follow the steps in sequence. Basically, you need two elements:
(a) the future tense of **být** (shown below)
(b) the infinitive of the imperfective verb you want to use (easy – because you already know it or can look it up)

The future tense of **být** is shown in the following table, alongside the present tense forms which you already know.

Singular				Plural		
Present		Future		Present		Future
I am	jsem	I will	**budu**	we are	jsme	we will **budeme**
you are	jsi	you will	**budeš**	you are	jste	you will **budete**
he is		he will				
she is	je	she will	**bude**	they are	jsou	they will **budou**
it is		it will				

Did you notice that the endings added to **bud-** are the same as the second conjugation verb endings?

All you need do now is select the correct form of the future tense of **být** and follow it with the infinitive of the imperfective you want to use. Thus:

"She will make curtains" requires:

(a) the third person singular future tense of **být**: **bude**
(b) the infinitive of "to make": **dělat**
(c) the accusative of "curtains": **záclony**

Bude dělat záclony.

15.4 Verbs: negatives

When the future tense is constructed as described above, it is often called the "compound future" because of the fact that it is composed of two parts. The **ne-** which we add when negating the verb is added to the future tense of **být**, and NOT to the imperfective infinitive. Thus, "I will not wait" is **Nebudu čekat**.

15.5 Reflexive se

When the reflexive **se** is involved, it is the <u>second</u> word in the clause. Thus, "We will not come back" is **Nebudeme se vracet.**

Exercise 15.2

Translate into Czech.

1   You (singular) will not understand.

2   He will work today.

3   They will not walk there.

4   I will not hurry.

5   Children, you will walk.

6   We will wait.

15.6 Summary of the system of present and future tenses

(a) Perfective verbs, then, express the future tense without doing anything more to them than conjugating in the normal way.

(b) Imperfective verbs, when conjugated, express the present.

(c) To express the future tense of an imperfective verb, you use the future tense of **být** together with the infinitive of the imperfective verb concerned.

Your next question is bound to be "when do I use the perfective and when do I use the imperfective?" It will help here if you think of the perfective as "complete" and the imperfective as "incomplete". This idea of completeness or otherwise applies to the timespan of the action expressed by the future tense. Here are a couple of examples:

(a) "I shall wait" [where the waiting is for an indefinite period or an indefinite number of times]: **Budu čekat**
"I shall wait for you" [i.e. until you arrive – a definite period]: **Počkám na tebe.**

In the first instance, you would use the imperfective because there is no definite time or event at which the waiting will end. In the second, you would use the perfective because there is an event which "completes" the waiting – your arrival.

(b) What shall I do today [without any mention of what specifically is to be done]: **Co** budu dělat dnes?
I shall do it soon [where the speaker is referring to a specific task or action]: **Udělám** to zítra.

In the first sentence, you use the imperfective because the expression is concerned more with the "doing" itself than with a finished action. In the second, the focus is on a specific action and the doing <u>of that action</u>. Again, you can see how the concept of "completeness" applies: in the first sentence, there is no thinking through to the end result of the action; the second expresses the idea that there is something particular which needs to be done <u>and finished</u>.

As you can see, it will be more usual to form future tenses with the perfective forms of verbs than with imperfectives. You should now be able to appreciate that, if you wish to show that an action or state in the future will be repeated or remain unfinished, you need the imperfective future. For example, "I shall be reading" or "I shall read" (without finishing or an indefinite number of times) is **Budu číst**. "I shall write a letter", however, is a once-only (it is "a" letter, not letters in general) and is thus a complete action. i.e. "I shall write a letter" (and then finish). For this, you need the perfective future: **Napíšu dopis**.

Exercise 15.3

Complete the sentences with the Czech translations of the English verbs given at the beginning of each sentence, being careful in your decision as to whether to use the perfective or imperfective.

1   to visit   Milane, ... Ivanu příští sobotu?

2   to wait   Pan Černý má hodně práce, ... dlouho.

3   to do   Neví, jak to udělat, asi to .... celé odpoledne.

4   to return   Snad (my) .... včas.

5   to eat   Tady máte tolik jídla! To .... celý týden. Ten tvarohový koláč je tak dobrý, že ho .... hned.

6   to see   Pojedeme tam už tento týden, tak malého Petra brzy ....

7   to look at; watch   Nemáme jiný program, ... celý večer na televizi.

8   to write   Chci .... ten dopis hned, pak už nebudu mít čas.

9   to get dressed   Pomůžu ti, až ....

10 to buy   Není tady nic k pití. Je tady jenom jedna láhev minerálky. Musím .... další.

Exercise 15.4

Now, as well as deciding which aspect to use, you should select a verb which is appropriate in each of the following sentences.

1 Vrací se brzy, ale dnes .... pozdě.

2 Nečte mnoho, ale tuto zajímavou knihu si jistě ....

3 Dnes mám velký hlad, tak se navečeřím, ale příští týden už ....

4 Vždy se rozhodují rychle, ale to je obtížná situace, ... dlouho.

5 Kupujeme pomeranče, ale pro vás .... jablka, když je máte rádi.

6 Neděláme zelený čaj, ale pro tebe ho ....

7 To je dlouhý text. Nemůžu se ho naučit, ... celé odpoledne.

15.7 Imperative of být

Now that you have learned the future tense of **být** here, as promised in paragraph 14.2, are the imperative forms of the verb which, as you can see, take the future tense as their basis. You will notice a similarity to **pojít** in the way the **d** acquires a háček (**d'**) and the **e** drops out.

			IMPERATIVES		
Infin	3rd person pl. (future tense)	Ending removed; háček added	2nd person singular	2nd person plural	1st person plural
být	budou	bud'	bud'	bud'te	bud'me

213

Vocabulary

ananas (*m*)	pineapple
borůvka (*f*)	bilberry
další	following; further; additional
dezert (*m*)	dessert
dívat se na	to look at
dort (*m*)	cake
dovnitř	inside
drůbež (*f*)	poultry
dušený	stewed
hovězí	beef (adjective)
hranolky (*pl*)	chips
chutnat	to taste
chvilka (*f*)	a short while
jablko (*n*)	apple
jahoda (*f*)	strawberry
ještě jednou	once more
kachna (*f*)	duck
kávový dort (*m*)	coffee cake
koláč (*m*)	cake; tart; pie
křen (*m*)	horseradish
lákavý	tempting
mandarinka (*f*)	tangerine
míchaný	mixed
minerálka (*f*)	mineral water
mít se hezky	to have a nice time (translate as "take care" in dialogue)
nápoj (*m*)	beverage
objednávka (*f*)	an order (when ordering a meal etc.)
obtížný	difficult
olej (*m*)	oil
palačinka (*f*)	pancake
pomeranč (*m*)	orange
pomoci	to help (this is, in effect, **moci** plus a prefix **po** which explains **pomůžu**)
pospíchat	to hurry (up); be in a hurry
pozdě	late
předkrm (*m*)	hors d'oeuvre; starter
příchuť (*f*)	taste; flavour
přípitek (*m*)	toast (as in "drink a toast", not grilled bread!)

příští	next; following
psát	to write (first person singular=**píšu**)
raději	rather; prefer (comes from root **mít rád**: the **-ěji** suffix, which denotes comparison, will be explained in Chapter 16)
rozhodnout	to decide; determine
rýže (*f*)	rice
sardinka (*f*)	sardine
situace (*f*)	situation
smažený	fried
smutný	sad
snad	perhaps; maybe; possibly
spokojený	satisfied
stihnout	to catch (first person singular=**stihnu**)
šlehačka (*f*)	whipped cream
talíř (*m*)	plate
text (*m*)	text
tvarohový	cream-cheese (adjective from **tvaroh** (*m*) cream cheese)
účet (*m*)	bill
úplné	fully; completely; absolutely
uprostřed	in the middle
vítat	to welcome
vybrat	to choose (first person singular=vyberu)
vývar (*m*)	broth; stock
zaplatit	to pay
zlatý	golden
zmrzlina (*f*)	ice-cream
zmrzlinový	pohár (*m*) ice-cream sundae
znova	again; once more

15.8 Dialogue

Finally, here is the dialogue, which you should work
through in the usual manner.

DIALOGUE

V restauraci

Karel: Podívej, Petře, to je úplné nová restaurace; jmenuje se "U zlatého jablka". Mám docela hlad. Půjdeme dovnitř a podíváme se, co nabízejí?

Petr: Ano, můžeme.

Waiter: Dobrý den. Vítáme vás. Chcete sedět u okna nebo raději uprostřed?

Karel: Dobrý den. Raději si sedneme k oknu. Děkujeme.

Waiter: Prosím, tady je jídelní lístek.

Waiter: Už jste si vybrali?

Petr: Já ano: vezmu si vepřovou, knedlík a zelí. Ale můj přítel si nemůže vybrat. Máte tolik lákavých jídel, tak vybírá a vybírá.

Karel: To je pravda. Dám si brambory a zeleninu, bez masa.

Waiter: Co si budete přát k pití?

Petr: Já samozřejmě pivo – a ty?

Karel: Dám si minerálku.

Waiter: Chutnalo vám? Nedáte si dezert?

Karel: Ano, bylo to dobré. Dám si ještě zmrzlinový pohár, s ovocem.

Waiter: Jaké ovoce si vyberete? Jahody, mandarinky, ananas, borůvky?

Karel: Ananas a taky kávu, prosím.

Waiter: Prosím.

Petr: Zaplatíme, prosím.

Waiter: Tady je účet, prosím. Byli jste spokojeni?

Petr: Ano, bylo to velmi dobré. Děkujeme, na shledanou.

Waiter: Na shledanou a těšíme se na vaši další návštěvu. Mějte se hezky.

Karel: Bylo to dobré a ne tak drahé. Kam půjdeme teď?

Petr: Můžeme se chvilku projít a pak půjdeme na výstavu!

TRANSLATION

In the restaurant

Karel: Look, Peter, there's a brand new restaurant. It's called "At the Golden Apple". I'm fairly hungry. Shall we go inside and see what they're offering?

Petr: Yes, we can.

Waiter: Good afternoon. Welcome. Would you like to sit at the window or in the centre [of the restaurant]?

Karel: Good afternoon. We'd prefer to sit at the window. Thank you.

Waiter: Not at all. Here is the menu.

Waiter: Are you ready to order? [literally, "Have you chosen?"]

Petr: Yes, I have: I'll have pork, dumplings and cabbage. But my friend can't choose. You've got so many tempting meals on offer he's choosing over and over again.

Karel: That's true. I'll have potatoes and vegetables without meat.

Waiter: What would you like to drink?

Petr: I'll have beer, of course – and you?

Karel: I'll have mineral water.

Waiter: Did you enjoy it? Will you have a dessert?

Karel: Yes, it was good. I'll have an ice-cream sundae with fruit.

Waiter: What kind of fruit will you have [lit., "choose"]? Strawberries, tangerines, pineapple, bilberries?

Karel: Pineapple, please and a coffee as well.

Waiter: With pleasure.

Petr: We'd like to pay now [lit., "We're going to pay now"].

Waiter: Here is the bill, thank you [lit., "please"]. Were you satisfied?

Petr: Yes, it was delicious. Thank you, goodbye.

Waiter: Goodbye. We look forward to your next visit. Take care.

Karel: That was good, and not too expensive. Where are we going now?

Petr: We can go for a short walk and then we'll go to see an exhibition.

Chapter 16

- *Nouns, adjectives and pronouns in the instrumental case*
- *Prepositions with the instrumental case*
- *Comparison of adjectives*
- *Verbal prefixes*

16.1 Nouns: instrumental case

Our seventh – and final – case! As its name implies, the instrumental case expresses the means by, or through which, an action is performed. If we tell you that the preposition which is most commonly used with the instrumental is **s** (or **se**) meaning "with" or "together with", you should begin to get the hang of it. For example, in "I went there with John", you would use the preposition **s** for "with" and the instrumental form of "John", which, as you can see from the table below, would be **Johnem**; thus: **Šel jsem tam s Johnem.** Now study the table below which compares the nominative forms with the instrumental ones.

	Hard		Soft	
Gender	Nom.	Instrumental	Nom.	Instrumental
Masc. animate	student	student**em**	muž	muž**em**
Masc. inanimate	most	most**em**	pokoj	pokoj**em**
Fem. ("a" or "e" ending)	žena	žen**ou**	židle	židl**í**
(consonant ending)	místnost	místnost**í**	skříň	skříň**í**
Neuter	město	měst**em**	moře	moř**em**
("e" or "i" ending)	náměstí	náměst**ím**	děvče	děvč**etem**

Another way of explaining the function of the instrumental case is by saying that it is used when the noun is the instrument or implement which is used to perform the action of the verb – for example, "I cut it with a knife" or, "I wrote with a pencil". "Knife" and "pencil" in these sentences would take the instrumental. However, because you denote the function of the noun by the very fact of using the instrumental, it is not always necessary to use a preposition as well. Let's take the example, "For this letter, I wrote with a pen". In English, "with" is essential to the meaning – try saying it without "with", and see how any sense we might make of it would probably be completely at odds with what the speaker is trying to say. But, because Czech carries the "with" or the "means-by-which" meaning within the instrumental case, the preposition is unnecessary: **Tento dopis jsem psala perem**. Similarly, "I went there by car" would be **Jel jsem tam autem**.

16.2 Adjectives: instrumental case

	Hard		Soft	
Gender	Nom.	Instrumental	Nom.	Instrumental
Masc. animate	velký	velký**m**	moderní	moderní**m**
Masc. inanimate	velký	velký**m**	moderní	moderní**m**
Feminine	velký	velk**ou**	moderní	moderní
Neuter	velký	velký**m**	moderní	moderní**m**

Exercise 16.1

Fill in the blanks in the following sentences with the correct forms of the words in brackets.

1   Mluvil jsem s (jeho přítel) ....

2   Šel tam s (Ivana a Pepík) ....

3   Jeli tam (auto) ....

4   Musíme tam jet (vlak) ....

5   Ještě neletěli (letadlo) ....

6   Můžete jet (tramvaj) .... nebo (metro) ....

7   Ten formulář vyplňte (pero) .... ne (tužka) ....

8   S (tenhle prací prostředek) .... to bude snadné.

9   Půjdeme (park) ...., to bude velmi příjemné.

10 Už to díte umí jíst (příbor) .... ?

16.3 Personal pronouns: instrumental case

The only comment which is required on the table which follows is on the third person forms of the pronouns. As you will see, there are two forms – one beginning with **n**, the other with **j**. The form beginning with **n** is the one which is used when the pronoun is preceded by a preposition (as it is in our table); the **j** form is used when there is no preposition, and so is just another example of the change from **j** to **n** with which you are already familiar when a preposition precedes the pronoun.

Singular				Plural			
Nom.		Instrumental		Nom.		Instrumental	
I	**já**	with me	**se mnou**	we	**my**	with us	**s námi**
you	**ty**	with you	**s tebou**	you	**vy**	with you	**s vámi**
he	**on**	with him	**s ním** (jím)		**oni**		
she	**ona**	with her	**s ní** (jí)	they	**ony**	with them	**s nimi** (jimi)
it	**ono**	with it	**s ním** (jím)		**ona**		

Exercise 16.2

Fill in the blanks.

1 Šli tam s rodiči? Ano, šli tam s ....

2 Mluvili jste s Janou? Ne, ještě jsme s .... nemluvili.

3 S kým tam chcete jet? S Petrem? Ano, s ....

4 Já to budu dělat. Budete pracovat se .... ?

5 Pojedeš taky? Rádi s .... pojedeme.

6 Už to víte. Vím, že s .... mluvili.

7 (my) Setkali se tam s ....

8 (vy) S .... jsme se už domluvili.

9 Počítám s (ty) .... i (oni) s ....

16.4 Demonstrative pronouns: instrumental case

Gender	Nominative	Instrumental
Masculine	toho/ten	**s tím**
Feminine	ta	**s tou**
Neuter	to	**s tím**

16.5 Possessive pronouns: instrumental case

	Masculine		Feminine		Neuter	
	Nom.	Inst.	Nom.	Inst.	Nom.	Inst.
my	můj	**mým**	má	**mou**	mé	**mým**
your	tvůj	tvým	tvá	**tvou**	tvé	tvým
his and its	jeho	jeho	jeho	jeho	jeho	jeho
hers	její	její	její	její	její	její
our	náš	**naším**	naše	**naší**	naše	**naším**
your	váš	vaším	vaše	**vaší**	vaše	vaším
their	jejich	jejich	jejich	jejich	jejich	jejich
reflexive	svůj	**svým**	svá	**svou**	své	**svým**

16.6 Prepositions with the instrumental case

You have already met **s** (**se**), but the following prepositions may also be used with the instrumental case. They are not, however, exclusive to it. Have a look at them and then we'll explain.

mezi	between
pod	under
za	behind; beyond
nad	above
před	in front of

Your first reaction to this may well be, "But I thought we'd use the locative with these prepositions, because they denote location, don't they?" Yes, they do – and you are quite right to think in that way. However, no two languages can ever parallel each other exactly so, despite what appears to be the English logic here, you must simply accept that these prepositions take the Czech instrumental when referring to position. Static position, that is. Because here's another rule that you need to know. These prepositions can also be used with the accusative case. The translation is the same, but the difference is this: when the words are used to denote not a static position, but a <u>movement in the relevant direction</u> (above, under, in front of, or behind) they are followed by the accusative, not the instrumental.

You should try to devise some way of remembering this. Here are a couple of suggestions:

(a) the instrumental is when you could answer the question "where <u>is</u> the noun <u>sitting</u>?" / "where does it <u>happen to be at this moment</u>?", while the accusative is used when your answer would be to the question, "where is the noun <u>moving to</u>?"

(b) another solution is to memorize a short phrase along the lines of "sitting <u>in</u> the <u>instrumental</u>; moving towards the accusative" and chant it to yourself parrot-fashion whenever this issue arises.

Compare the English and the Czech in the pairs of sentences in each of the two examples below.

(a) **Veverka sedí na stromě**. (The squirrel is sitting <u>in</u> the tree.) Here, the squirrel is sitting <u>in</u> the tree: the tree happens to be where it <u>is</u> – and it is showing no inclination to go anywhere else. The instrumental case is used. **Veverka leze <u>na</u> strom**. (The squirrel is climbing <u>into</u> the tree.) Here, the squirrel is <u>moving</u> from one place to another. The accusative case is used.

(b) **Lampa visí <u>nad</u> stolem**. (The lamp is hanging above the table.) The verb "is hanging" tells us where the lamp <u>is</u> – it's above the table <u>now</u> and for the foreseeable future. The instrumental is used.
Dali lampu <u>nad</u> stůl. (They put the lamp above the table.) At the time we are talking about, "they" were <u>moving</u> the lamp from one place to another – the idea here is of a lamp <u>in transit</u>. The accusative is used.

16.7 Comparison of adjectives

Until now, we have used adjectives only in their positive form, such as "old", "new", "young" and so on. By comparison of adjectives, we mean the forms we use when we want to make a comparison between one thing and another: for example, "older", "newer", "younger". That form of the adjective is, unsurprisingly, called the comparative. Finally, there are the forms "oldest", "newest", "youngest": these are the superlative forms.

16.8 Comparison of adjectives: first group

To construct comparative and superlative adjectives, Czech follows a procedure which is not dissimilar to English – by adapting the positives. One of the most usual ways in which to form the comparative is to remove the ending (-ý or -í) and add the suffix -ější or -ejší to the stem of the positive:

Positive	Remove stem	Comparative
nový	nov-	novější
moderní	modern-	modernější
rychlý	rychl-	rychlejší

So, to say, "The Metro is faster than a tram": **Metro je rychlejší než tramvaj.**

Look again at the comparative forms above, and notice how they all end in -í – the soft adjective ending. This means that an adjective whose positive form was hard becomes soft in the comparative and is declined as a soft adjective. In other words, the comparative of **nový** (**novější**) is declined on the **moderní** pattern in all cases.

The superlative is formed by adding the prefix **nej-** to the comparative, as shown below.

Positive	Comparative	Superlative
nový	novější	**nej**novější
moderní	modernější	**nej**modernější
rychlý	rychlejší	**nej**rychlejší

So, "The Metro is the fastest means of transport in Prague":
Metro je nejrychlejší dopravní prostředek v Praze.

16.9 Comparison of adjectives: second group

This set of adjectives forms comparatives by adding just **-ší** to the stem. Having found the comparative, however, the superlative simply involves the addition of the **nej-** prefix as above.

Positive	Remove stem	Comparative	Superlative
starý	star-	star**ší**	**nej**starší
mladý	mlad-	mlad**ší**	nejmlad**ší**

The next table of adjectives follows this same basic pattern although, as you will notice, there are consonant changes. Don't spend time on working out or memorizing the consonant changes – we have included these adjectives only because they are ones you are quite likely to want to use.

Positive	Remove stem → change consonant	Comparative	Superlative
blízký	blíz → ž	bli**žší**	**nej**bližší
drahý	drah → ž	dra**žší**	nejdra**žší**
tichý	tich → š	ti**šší**	nejti**šší**

One consonant change which is consistent, however, is **-ký** to **-čí**, as in:

Positive	Remove stem	Comparative	Superlative
hezký	hez-	hez**čí**	**nej**hezčí
lehký	leh-	leh**čí**	**nej**lehčí

Exercise 16.3

Adjectives are given in brackets in their positive forms, but the positive form does not make sense in the sentence. Use the comparative or superlative form, as appropriate, to fill the gaps.

1   Nevím, co je (rychlý) .... jet metrem nebo auto-busem?

2   Karlův most je (starý) .... most v Praze.

3   V tomto obchodě je všechno (drahý) .... než v tom malém blízko našeho domu.

4   Petr je jejich (starý) .... syn, mají také Milana a ten je (mladý) ....

5   To je asi (důležitý) .... ze všeho.

6   Který obraz je (hezký) .... ?

7   Tahle kniha je (zajímavý) .... ze všech, co jsem četl.

8   Který z nich je (mladý) ....? Honza nebo Pepa?

9   Byl to (krásný) .... koncert z celého festivalu.

16.10 Comparison of adjectives: irregular adjectives

Although it's not much consolation, do bear in mind that English has its irregular adjectives too. Consider: "it's a bad situation". To express the idea that something is "more than bad", we don't say "badder", but "worse" – nor do we say "baddest", but "worst". The comparative and superlative forms here are not formed from the positive. Here are some of the more common Czech irregular adjectives, all of which you have met already in their positive forms (and the first of which, you will realize, is the very example we have just used in English).

Positive	Comparative	Superlative
špatný	horší	nejhorší
dobrý	lepší	nejlepší
velký	větší	největší
malý	menší	nejmenší
dlouhý	delší	nejdelší
hodně	více	nejvíce

Exercise 16.4

Do exacly the same with this exercise as with Exercise 16.3. Some of the questions involve the irregular adjectives you have just met; others belong to one or other of the regular sets.

1 Marie je (dobrý) .... studentka naší třídy.

2 Nevím, co je (špatný) ....

3 Nemůžeme tam být před nimi. Jejich auto je (rychlý) ....

4 To, co udělal, bylo (dobrý) ....

5 Děkuji ti za tu knihu, byla to (zajímavý) .... kniha, jakou jsem kdy četl.

6 Co je (lehký) ....? Učit se česky nebo anglicky?

7 Miss Čechy je (hezký) dívka Čech.

8 Ta černá sukně je (malý) .... než ta šedá.

9 Musíme hledat nějaké (praktický) .... řešení.

16.11 Comparison of adjectives: final word

You may be wondering how you identify the group to which any given adjective belongs. This is something which even native Czechs find difficult, and is beyond the scope of this course. For practical purposes, we suggest that you make sure that you thoroughly understand, and can apply, the rules we have taught you above but, if in doubt, add the -**ější** ending: as we have stressed throughout the course, it is better to say something which will probably be sufficient to be understood, even if it is not one hundred percent correct, than to stare dumbstruck as you try to rack your brains for the right ending. "Having a go" <u>shows</u> that you have made, and are making, an effort with the language, but opening and shutting your mouth like a fish really does look idiotic!! If you feel <u>really</u> stuck – you're still getting a blank stare – another (ungrammatical and last-ditch) possibility would be to avoid the comparatives altogether by putting a word such as **hodně** or **moc** in front of the positive form; for example, **Auto je rychlé, ale Metro je hodně rychlé**.

16.12 Verbal prefixes

We have met verbal prefixes before. In Lesson 12, we saw how a prefix could change the <u>aspect</u> of the verb from imperfective to perfective – for example, **děkovat** → **poděkovat, platit** → **zaplatit, číst** → **přečíst** etc.; in Chapter 13, we saw that prefixes are added to the verbs of motion to form the future tense. Here, we are concerned with verbal prefixes which alter the meaning of the verb itself. English too has verbal prefixes in this sense: consider "<u>un</u>do", "<u>dis</u>-connect", "<u>re</u>view", and you probably wouldn't have too much difficulty explaining the general effect of "un-", "dis-" and "re-" to someone who was learning English. But how would you cope with "to take over" in relation to "take" and "to bite back" in relation to "to bite"? These compound verbs of ours cause problems to foreign learners – and Czech too has its fair share of compound verbs as well as those which have just had a stock prefix added. In the following paragraphs we will introduce some of the standard prefixes and, where appropriate, introduce some of the compound verbs whose construction is less transparent.

16.13 *při-*

The prefix **při-**expresses movement <u>towards</u> the object or the speaker: $- - - - - - \rightarrow \bigcirc$.

Thus: from **jít** and **jet**, you find <u>při</u>**jít** and <u>při</u>**jet**; (to come <u>towards</u>), from **nést** (to carry), <u>při</u>**nést** (to bring); from **svařit** (to weld), you find <u>při</u>**vařit** (to weld on) and from **sedět** (to sit) you also have <u>při</u>**sednout** (to sit down next to, to join someone). Here are two that aren't as obvious: you know that "to get up" is **vstát** – "to get up extra early" is <u>při</u>**vstát**; "to stir" is **míchat** and "to stir in" is <u>při</u>**míchat**.

All in all, then, the prefix **při-** denotes the addition of something to the main verb. It can be used with nouns too. Examples include:

<u>při</u>**jezd** (*m*)	arrival
<u>pří</u>**let** (*m*)	flight arrival
<u>pří</u>**chod** (*m*)	arrival on foot

all of which should be quite clear. Others, though, are more obscure: **chuť** (*f*) means "taste", or "flavour" and we have **příchuť** (*f*) which is added taste or flavour and, with **přípitek** (*m*) which means "a toast", we really are getting into the workings of the language. You know all the words necessary to follow this through, though, so here's a taste: **pít** (to drink) → **připít** (to drink <u>towards</u> – thus, "towards a person") → **přípitek** (*m*) toast (!).

Constructions like this are beyond the scope of this course but, as we've emphasized throughout, the more you're aware of the elements of which the language is made up, the more likely you are to be able to have a stab at understanding a word which is, at first sight, completely unknown to you.

16.14 Od-/ode-

The prefix **od-/ode** expresses movement <u>away from</u> the object or the speaker: ← – – – – –O.

Thus: **odejít** and **odjet** mean "to leave", **odnést** means "to carry away" and **odepsat** means "to write back" (remember the direction of movement is away from the <u>speaker</u>). And the meaning of the nouns **odjezd** (*m*), **odlet** (*m*) and **odchod** (*m*) should, we would hope, be clear by analogy with their equivalents with the prefix **při-** above.

Exercise 16.5

Use what you have learned about the verbal prefixes to fill in the blanks in the following sentences.

1 Až zítra .... má přítelkyně, budu šťastný, až za týden .... budy smutný.

2 Už nebudete jíst? Můžu .... ten talíř a .... zmrzlinu?

3 Připravuje pro vás kávu. Už ji ....

4 Ten autobus už nestihneme. Právě tamhle ....

5 Počkám na tebe. Kdy ....? V deset?

6 Už musíme jet na letiště. Jejich .... má být ve 4 hodiny.

7 Nemusíte spěchat. Vlak .... až ve dvě hodiny.

16.15 Verbal prefixes involving other directions of movement

(a) **Vy-**
The prefix **vy-** means "out of" or "up", so "to go up", "to start" or (less obviously, perhaps) "to appear" can be expressed by **vyjít** or **vyjet**.

(b) **s-** or **se-**
The prefix **s-** (or **se-**) means "down" or "together", so **sejít** (**se**) and **sjet** mean "to go down" or "to meet".

(c) **do-**
The prefix **do-** expresses the reaching of a destination or goal – again, its use is most immediately apparent in relation to the verbs of motion.

Exercise 16.6

Fill in the prefixes in the following sentences.

1   Včera jsme se .....šli s Ivanou, procházeli jsme se po Praze a .....šli jsme až na Vyšehrad. Byla to hezká procházka.

2   I když tam nebyl výtah, ...šli jsme až nahoru.

3   Už tady nejsou, ...šli včera.

4   Když jsem ji uviděl, právě .....cházela z kina.

5   .....šli jsme až do cíle, ale byli jsme unaveni.

6   Ty noviny .....cházejí také v neděli?

7   .....jíždíš tam každý den?

8   Nevíš, kdy .....jíždí ten večerní autobus?

9   Pospěš si! Autobus .....jíždí za čtvrt hodiny.

10 Až si prohlédnete všechny místnosti tady nahoře, můžete .....jít dolů.

16.16 Prefixes *ob-/obe-; pro-*

(a) **ob-/obe-**
This prefix indicates <u>going around</u> or <u>circumventing</u> something or someone. For example, **Nerad chodím v noci parkem**. (I don't like walking <u>through</u> the park at night.) **Vždy ho radši <u>obe</u>jdu**. (I prefer to <u>avoid</u> it. i.e. by "walking <u>round</u>" it.)

Jsem obřezaný. (I am circumcised.) **Obřezaný** is an adjective which is derived from the verb **řezat** (to cut); thus, <u>**obřezat**</u> means "to cut <u>around</u> (and off)".

Můj manžel chrápe jen občas. (My husband snores only occasionally. i.e. "<u>around</u> time".)

(b) **pro-**
This prefix expresses "through", so one of the circumstances in which you may well meet it is, again, with the verbs of motion. Thus, <u>**projít**</u> and <u>**projet**</u>. More interestingly from the linguistic point of view, and more usefully if you are being given instructions in the kitchen by a Czech friend, is **povařit** which comes from **vařit** (to cook). "Through-cook"? You'd be almost there – **povařit** means "to cook gently for a while" or, as our recipe books might say, "simmer".

Exercise 16.7

Try translating this short passage about a train journey in which ample use is made of the verbal prefixes.

Vlak vyjel z nádraží. Jel chvíli po rovině, pak vyjel na kopec, sjel zas dolů, a projel tunelem. Když vyjel z tunelu, nadjel řeku a podjel vysoký most. Nakonec dojel na nádraží.

Vocabulary

akvizice *(f)*	takeover
balení *(n)*	packaging
bezvýznamný	insignificant
cena *(f)*	price
cíl *(m)*	aim; goal
cítit se	to feel
co si to dovolujete!	how dare you!
cože	but
dlouhovlasý	long-haired
dopravní prostředek *(m)*	means of transport
důležitý	important
ekonomik *(f)*	economics
fanatik *(m)*	fanatic
festival *(m)*	festival
formulář	form
holt	just
hospodárnost *(f)*	economy
chmel *(pl)*	hops
chutnat	to taste
Jánošík *(m)*	is a Slovak folk-hero – a bit like Robin Hood
je vidět	it's obvious
kapsa *(f)*	pocket
kříž(ek) *(m)*	(little) cross
kvalitní	top-quality
laciný	cheap; inexpensive
letadlo *(n)*	aeroplane
lézt to	climb
například	for example; for instance
navíc	besides
několik	some; a few
neporovnatelně	incomparably
nezáleží	less important
nežli	than
objevit	to discover; find out
obsah *(m)*	contents
odkud *(adv)*	where .... from
pivovar *(m)*	brewery
počítat s	to count; to take into account
podepsat	to sign

podnik (*m*)	enterprise; undertaking; business
pokrok (*m*)	progress
po rovině (*adv*)	straight
poučit se	to learn
prací prostředek (*m*)	detergent
prodiskutovat	to discuss
prostředek (*m*)	means; facility; tool
průzkum (*m*)	research; investigation
prvotřídní	first-class
přece	all the same; yet; though in fact
převézt	to take over
příbor (*m*)	cutlery
rozmyslit si	to think over; reconsider
řádka (*f*)	line
řešení (*n*)	solution
řizení (*n*)	control; management; direction
setkat se	to meet
smlouva (*f*)	contract
snížit	to bring down; cut (price)
stačit	be enough
strkat	to shove; push; thrust
tunel (*m*)	unnel
úsilí (*n*)	drive; effort
úspěšný	successful
věřit	to believe
veverka (*f*)	squirrel
viset	to hang
vlak (*m*)	train
výtah (*m*)	lift; elevator
vytečkovaný	dotted
základní	elementary
zde	we
zpátky (*adv*)	back; backwards
zpívat	to sing
zůstat	to stay; remain; stick

16.17 Dialogue

DIALOGUE

A: Dobrý den. Moc mě těší. Jak víte, přijeli jsme prodiskutovat naši akvizici vašeho bezvýznamného malého pivovaru.

B: Náš pivovar je přece známý po celém světě!

A: Možná několika dlouhovlasým fanatikům. Ale až převézmeme řízení podniku my, jméno piva JÁNOŠÍK si bude každý zpívat! Nemusí *chutnat* tak jak ted', samozřejm . . . .

B: Cože?

A: Náš průzkum objevil, že pivo se prodává úspešným balením. Na obsahu už tolik nezáleží.

B: Ale přece . . . .

A: Navíc, naším nejdůležitějším úsilím musí být hospodárnost. V první řadě musíme snížit ceny. Kolik vás, například, stojí tenhle prvotřídní chmel?

B: Zde v JÁNOŠÍKU věříme, že kvalitní chmel je to, co . . . .

A: Kvalita? No prosím! Vy nerozumíte ani základům ekonomiky.

B: Promiňte, ale tenhle dražší chmel chutná neporovnatelně lépe nežli kdejaký laciný.

A: Milý pane, tady jde o obchod.

B: Myslím, že si nerozumíme.

A: Nebojte se. Naši právníci už napsali smlouvy, stačí jen podepsat – tady na té vytečkované řádce . . . .

B: To nemohu!

A: No, tak tam jen udělejte křížek . . . .

B: Co si to dovolujete! Vite, co s tím svým perem můžete udělat? Strčte si ho zpátky do kapsy a jděte si zpátky odkud jste přišel. My zůstaneme u toho, v co věříme.

A: Je vidět, že nevěříte v pokrok. No, zavolejte mi, až si to rozmyslíte.

B: Nikdy.

A: No jo. Někteří lidě se holt nikdy nepoučí.

TRANSLATION

A: Good morning. Nice to meet you. As you know, we came here to discuss our takeover of your insignificant little brewery.

B: But our brewery is famous the world over!

A: To some few long-haired fanatics, maybe. But when we take over the running of the company, the name JANOSIK lager will be on everyone's lips. It needn't *taste* the same, of course . . . .

B: What?

A: Our research has found that it's successful packaging that sells beer. The contents are less important.

B: Oh, but . . . .

A: Besides, the most important drive for us will be economy. First, we must get the price down. How much do these first-class hops cost you, for example?

B: We at JANOSIK believe in the importance of good-quality hops, and . . . .

A: Quality? Exactly! You simply don't understand elementary economics.

B: With respect, the expensive hops taste incomparably better than the cheap ones.

A: My dear man, we're running a business here.

B: I don't think we understand each other.

A: Don't worry. Our lawyers have already written the contracts, all you need to do is sign here on the dotted line . . . .

B: I can't do that!

A: Well, just mark it with an "x" here . . . .

B: How dare you! You know what you can do with your pen? Shove it back in your pocket, and go back where you came from. We'll stick to what we believe in.

A: Obviously, you don't believe in progress. Well, ring me when you reconsider.

B: Never.

A: Oh, well. Some people just never learn.

Chapter 17

- *Nouns, adjectives and pronouns in the locative plural*
- *Comparison of adverbs*
- *Verbs: the conditional mood*
- *The conjunction* **aby**

17.1 Nouns: the locative plural

By now, you should be familiar with the format! Here are the locative plurals alongside their singular forms.

Gender	Singular	Plural	Singular	Plural
Masc. animate	o studentovi OR o studentu	o studentech	o mužovi OR o muži	o mužích
Masc. inanimate	o mostu OR o mostě	o mostech	o pokoji	o pokojích
Fem. ("a" or "e" ending)	o ženě	o ženách	o židli	o židlích
(consonant ending)	v místnosti	v místnostech	o skříni	o skříních
Neuter	ve městě OR o městu	ve městech	o moři	o mořích
("e" or "i" ending)	o náměstí	o náměstích	o děvčeti	o děvčatech

If you look back at the vocabulary for Exercise 8.1, you'll see that Christmas (**vánoce**) and Easter (**velikonoce**) are feminine plural nouns. So, to say "at Christmas" and "at Easter", you would need the locative plural <u>and</u> a capital letter: o **Vánocích**; o **Velikonocích**.

The names of some cities are also plural in form – for example, Poděbrady (f) and Teplice (f). To say "at" these places, you need the locative plural: v **Poděbradech**, v **Teplicích**.

17.2 Adjectives: locative plural

As with the dative, you need learn only two rules, and these two rules apply to all genders:

(a) hard adjectives add -**ých** to the stem – thus nový becomes nov**ých**
(b) soft adjectives add -**ích** to the stem – thus moderní becomes modern**ích**.

17.3 Demonstrative pronouns: locative case

Gender	Singular	Plural
Masculine	o tom	o **těch**
Feminine	o té	o **těch**
Neuter	o tom	o **těch**

17.4 Possessive pronouns: locative case

	Masculine		Feminine		Neuter	
	Singular	Plural	Singular	Plural	Singular	Plural
my	o mém	o m**ých**	o mé	o m**ých**	o mém	o m**ých**
your	o tvém	o tv**ých**	o tvé	o tv**ých**	o tvém	o tv**ých**
his and its	o jeho	o jeho	o jeho	o jeho	o jeho	o jeho
hers	o jejím	o jej**ích**	o její	o jej**ích**	o jejím	o jej**ích**
our	o našem	o naš**ich**	o naší	o naš**ich**	o našem	o naš**ich**
your	o vašem	o vaš**ich**	o vaší	o vaš**ich**	o vašem	o vaš**ich**
their	o jejich	o jejich	o jejich	o jejich	o jejich	o jejich
reflexive	o svém	o sv**ých**	o své	o sv**ých**	o svém	o sv**ých**

Exercise 17.1

Put the expressions in brackets into the locative plural.

1 Mluvili jsme o (vaši noví přátelé) ....

2 Nerad jím v (restaurace) ...., nerad bydlím v (hotely) ....

3 Ráno je v (ulice) .... města velký provoz.

4 V (ty pokoje) .... je také koupelna.

5 Na (všechny židle) .... je plno věcí. Kdo to uklidí?

6 Chceme o (vaše problémy) .... něco vědět.

7 Znal příběhy snad o (všechny místa) .... v Praze.

8 Na (velká náměstí) .... jsou parky.

9 Ve (staré domy) .... nejsou výtahy.

10 Záleží také na (jejich názory) ....

11 Po (Vánoce) .... zase přijdeme.

12 O (Velikonoce) ...... jezdíme ven.

13 Potkali jsme se o dovolené v (Poděbrady) ....

14 Každý rok je v (Domažlice) .... festival.

17.5 Comparison of adverbs

This is very similar to the comparison of adjectives which we did in Chapter 16. Bearing in mind that an adverb is to a verb what an adjective is to a noun – adjectives tell you "what sort of" thing the noun is; adverbs tell you "the way in which" the action of the verb is performed – and the fact that Czech adverbs derive from adjectives, you will not be surprised to see that many features of comparison are the same. The method of forming the comparatives is broadly similar, as are the groups into which they fall; the way in which the superlative is formed from the comparative is identical, and there is also a fair crop of irregular adverbs. Because of these affinities, we shall deal with this topic fairly rapidly. If you don't feel comfortable with this pace, have another look at adverbs in paragraphs 13.5–13.7 and at the comparison of adjectives in paragraphs 16.7–16.11.

17.6 Comparison of adverbs: first group

Look at the table below and try to work out how the comparative and superlative forms are constructed. As usual, we have tried to highlight the changes through the use of **bold** type.

Positive	Remove stem	Comparative	Superlative
krásně	krásn-	krásn**ěji**	**nej**krásn**ěji**
pomalu	pomal-	pomal**eji**	**nej**pomal**eji**
rychle	rychl-	rychl**eji**	**nej**rychl**eji**
teplo	tepl-	tepl**eji**	**nej**tepl**eji**
tiše	tiš-	tiš**eji**	**nej**tiš**eji**
vesele	vesel-	vesel**eji**	**nej**vesel**eji**
zdravě	zdrav-	zdrav**ěji**	**nej**zdrav**ěji**

First of all, notice how the procedure of (a) removing the stem, (b) adding a suffix to form the comparison, and (c) adding the prefix **nej-** to form the superlative is identical to the process for adjectives. Next, look at the suffix added to the stem to make the comparative – there are two differences here: first, there is no **š**; second, the "i" is short (**i**) rather than long (**í**).

Our advice when you're not sure of the comparative form of an adverb is, again as with the adjectives, to try forming it in this way as a first attempt.

17.7 Comparison of adverbs: second group

Again, have a go at working out what's going on here:

Positive	Stem removed – and (consonant _and_ vowel changed if necessary)	Comparative	Superlative
blízko	blíz → ž	blíže	**nej**blíže
daleko	da → á	dále	**nej**dále
nízko	níz → ž	níže	**nej**níže
vysoko	vy → ý s → š	výše	**nej**výše

OK. Aside from the fact that we can ignore the superlative since it acts true to form with its **nej-** prefix, can we fathom out any rules for this group? Well, a common factor is that all of the adverbs here end in **-o**, **-eko**, or **-oko**. First, this ending drops off, leaving a stem. Second, if the vowel is not already long (as it is in **blízko** and **nikdo**, for example) it lengthens. Third, the final consonant of the stem softens – as it did in a number of adjectives in the second group (paragraph 16.9). Finally, an **e** is added.

With practice, what looks like a convoluted process will come naturally to you. It is because you may not have had <u>enough</u> practice by the time you first have to form one of them that we recommend that your first attempt in cases of doubt is the **-eji** or **-ěji** suffix method in paragraph 17.6 above!

An adverb which falls broadly within this second group, but is a bit of an oddball, is **snadno** (easily). Because it is so common, and you may well wish to use it, here it is:

Positive	Comparative	Superlative
snadno	sn**áze**	**nej**snáze

17.8 Comparison of adverbs: irregular adverbs

Again, although we can't anticipate all the irregular adverbs you might want to use, here are more or less the same ones as we included in the section on adjectives.

Positive	Comparative	Superlative
brzo	dříve	nejdříve
dlouho	déle	nejdéle
dobře	lépe	nejlépe
málo	méně	nejméně
mnoho	více	nejvíce
špatně	hůře	nejhůře

Exercise 17.2

The positive forms of the adverbs which are given in brackets do not make sense within the sentences. Use the comparative or superlative form, as appropriate, to fill the gaps. (You will find that one of the adverbs is not included in any of the above lists. Do what you think you should . . . !)

1   Už je před námi! Jeho auto jede (rychle) .... než naše.

2   Napsal to (dobře) .... z nás.

3   Včera jí bylo (špatně) .... než dnes.

4   Které dítě hodilo ten míč (daleko) ....?

5   Mluvil velmi dlouho, asi (dlouho) .... ze všech.

6   Když jedeme na výlet, musíme vstát (brzo) .... než obvykle.

7   Dnes přišla (pozdě) .... ze všech.

8   Ta expedice se dostala (daleko) .... ze všech.

17.9 Verbs: conditional mood

The conditional mood expresses the idea that one <u>could</u> or <u>would</u> do something as opposed to <u>is</u> doing something. Look at the following four examples. Notice first how the conditional mood is a form of expression which we use frequently in everyday English, and then see if you could explain to someone else why we use the term "conditional mood": (1) "I <u>would</u> go"; (2) "You <u>should</u> do it!"; (3) "She <u>could</u> help you"; (4) "We <u>should</u> go back".

In each case, there is no certainty that the people involved are doing, or will do these things – they are <u>conditional</u> on something else happening, or on some (as yet unknown) <u>conditions</u> being fulfilled. (In the context of an entire conversation, these conditions would, of course, become apparent.) This is not the only use of the conditional mood, as you may already realize, but before getting any deeper let's see how we form these expressions in Czech. We need two elements:

(a) the <u>-l</u> <u>participle</u> of the main verb (which, in the examples above, is "go", "do", "help" and "go back" respectively). As with the past tense, the -l participle must agree in <u>number</u> and <u>gender</u> with the subject of the sentence. These forms are set out for you in full in paragraph 9.1. In summary:

Singular:	masculine	no additional ending required
	feminine	add **a**
	neuter	add **o**
Plural:	masc. animate	add **i**
	masc. inanimate	add **y**
	feminine	add **y**
	neuter	add **a**

If you feel at all blank on this, go back to paragraph 9.1.

(b) the <u>conditional mood</u> of **být** – which takes
the following form:

Singular		Plural	
I	**bych**	we	**bychom**
you	**bys**	you	**byste**
he she it	**by**	they	**by**

Taking each of our examples above, then, we can work them
out as follows:

(1) "I would go" (assume that the speaker is a woman). We
    need:
    (a) the -l participle of the verb "to go" which is **šel** <u>plus</u>
    the feminine ending **-a** which, as you already know,
    gives us **šla;**
    (b)the first person singular of the conditional mood of
    být which is **bych.**
    Thus: **šla bych.**

(2) "You should do it" (assume two men are being
    addressed). We need:
    (a) the -l participle of the verb "to do" which is **dělal**
    <u>plus</u> the masculine plural ending **i** which gives us **dělali;**
    (b) the second person plural of the conditional mood of
    být which is **byste.**
    Thus: **dělali byste.**

(3) "She could help you." We need:
    (a) the -l participle of the verb "to help" which is
    pomohl <u>plus</u> the feminine ending **-a** which gives us
    pomohla;
    (b) the third person singular of the conditional mood of
    být which is **by.**
    Thus: **pomohla by (vám).**

(4) "We should go back" (assume that the group is com-
    prised of men and women). We need:
    (a) the -l participle of the verb "to go back" which is

vrátit se <u>plus</u> the <u>masculine</u> plural ending **-a** which gives us **vrátili se**;
(b) the first person plural of the conditional mood of **být** which is **bychom**. But because this is a reflexive verb, (b) comes between the -l participle and the reflexive **se**. Thus: **vrátili bychom se**.

And here is another point about reflexives. As you have just seen, the conditional mood of **být** comes between the -l participle and the reflexive **se**. There is one small change in the second person singular here: instead of the **vrátil bys se** which you would expect, you have **vrátil by ses** – the **s** is moved to the end. This is to facilitate understanding in the spoken language; it is the "s" sound which distinguishes the second from the third person singular and, without moving it on to the end of **se**, that sound would be lost.

17.10 Word order with the conditional mood

The rules here are exactly the same as those which applied in the past tense (see paragraph 9.3), but with the difference that it is the <u>conditional</u> mood of **být**, instead of its present tense, which is always the second element in the sentence or clause. As with the past tense, it is often the use of a pronoun which occasions the shift. Look at this example:

Šel <u>bych</u> tam; ty <u>bys</u> šel také? I would go there; would you go too?

If, of course, you wanted to emphasize yourself through the use of the first person pronoun, the first clause of your sentence would be **Já bych šel tam.**

Exercise 17.3

Before you complete the following sentences using the conditional mood, have a look at question 4. You haven't met **takhle** *before, but you will no doubt recognize its similarity to* **tohle** *. It means "like so" or "like this".* **Tak** *is an adverb which means "so; thus" and the addition of* **hle** *emphasizes it in the same way as it adds emphasis to* **to**. *So:*

Jak? (How?) – **Tak.** (So – *i.e.* like that.)
Jak? (How?) – **Takhle.** (This – *particular* – way.)
Dělám to tak dobře? (Am I doing this right?)
    – **Ne. Takhle je to lepší.** (No. This (way) is better.)

1   Koupil bys to? (já) .... také.

2   Zeptala by se a my .... také.

3   Udělal by to a oni .... také.

4   Dělal by to takhle a my .... také tak.

5   Ukázal by vám cestu, ale my .... také.

17.11 Use of the conditional mood to make a polite request

So far, we have used the conditional to express a state of affairs which has some uncertainty about it – some <u>condition</u> has to be fulfilled before "would" or "should" can become real action (if indeed they ever do). The conditional is also used to express a request politely. In English, there is a subtle difference between "will you give me that book" and "would you give me that book" which might almost be described as a difference in <u>attitude</u>. It is that (more respect-ful, or less aggressive) difference in attitude that you can convey by means of the conditional mood. Look at the following short dialogue and its translation, noting how the conditional mood softens the questions in which it is used.

A: Prosím vás, <u>nepůjčil byste</u> mi ten telefonní seznam?
B: Samozřejme, prosím.

Za chvíli

B: <u>Mohl bych</u> vám pomoci? Jaké číslo hledáte?
A: Děkuji, jste velice laskav.

TRANSLATION

A: Excuse me, <u>would you lend</u> me that telephone directory?
B: Of course, here you are.

After a while

B: <u>Could I</u> help you? What number are you looking for?
A: Thank you, that's very kind of you.

Here are a few more examples which you may wish to use.
Don't learn them just as phrase-book phrases, but pay attention to the construction of the conditional mood so that you will be able to convert requests into this polite form should you feel that the occasion demands it.

"We would like to stay here for five days" when making a reservation for accommodation is more polite than "We want to . . .". Thus: **Chtěli bychom zde zůstat asi pět dní.**

"I would like to know how much that costs": **Rád(a) bych věděl(a), kolik to stojí.**

"Would that be possible?": **Bylo by to možné?**

"Would you wait for a while?": **Počkali(y) byste chvíli?**

And finally, look at how the negative is used in this sentence:

Neřekl byste to ještě jednou? Literally, this is, "Wouldn't you say it once more?"; this has a note of supplication which implies that you are beholden to the person to whom you are addressing the request. You should be aware, though, that while this negative construction is used frequently in requests framed in the second and third persons, you should not use it with the first person. Thus, our example above – **Rád(a) bych věděl(a)** . . . would <u>not</u> be re-framed **Nerád(a) bych věděl(a).** . . .

Exercise 17.4

Use each expression to form a polite request. You may use either the positive or the negative form, bearing in mind what we've just said about negative constructions and the first person. The pronouns given in brackets tell you which person you should use, but you should omit them from the requests you construct.

1   (ty) Pomoci mi.

2   (ty) Podat tu knihu.

3   (vy) Jít tam taky.

4   (já) Vrátit se dřív.

5   (vy) Přijít k nám.

6   (ty) Půjčit ten časopis.

7   (oni) Zavřít okno.

8   (ty) Otevřít dveře.

17.12 The conjunction *aby*

The first thing to note is that **aby** is connected with the conditional mood. It is used with the -l participle and, effectively, it conjugates in the same way as the conditional mood of **být**.

Consider the following sentence: "He said I should come back". If someone were to say this to you it could mean one of two things. It could mean: "He said, 'I should come back' " meaning that "I should come back" were the words that issued from the third party's mouth (i.e. that the third party ("He") was referring to himself and his own possible return). Alternatively, it could mean that the speaker was saying that that a third party told the speaker that the speaker ("I") should return. In writing, the punctuation makes clear which of these two meanings is intended; in speech, you would probably know from the context. In the sentence you were asked to consider above, the punctuation makes clear that the second meaning is intended – "He" refers to a third party, and that third party was telling the speaker that he (the speaker, "I") should come back.

To make this clear in English speech, we might well say, "He said <u>that</u> I should come back". In Czech, this clarity is achieved by the use of **aby: Řekl, <u>abych</u> se vrátil**. Let's have a look at this.

We begin with the past tense of "he said" (**Řekl).** We then have to deal with "I should come back". "I should come back" on its own would be **Já bych se vrátil** (assuming you are a man) or **vrátil bych se** if you didn't want to use the pronoun. But this sets up the same ambiguity as we highlighted in our English sentence. The use of **aby** clarifies the situation.

As we implied above, **aby** changes according to who is performing the action of the verb in the subordinate clause, and it takes the same endings as the conditional form of **být.** Let's look at a few more examples.

"He said she should go there." Begin by looking at what really is being said. This is the same construction as our previous example, so what the speaker means is, "He said that she should go there". The "He said" part is **Řekl** as you would expect; "she should go there" as a sentence on its own would be **šla by tam**, but we want to incorporate the idea of "that" or indirect speech so we need **aby.** "She" is the third person feminine so, given that **aby** takes the same endings as the conditional mood of **být,** we have **aby.** However, just as the conditional mood element is always the second element in the sentence, so is **aby.** So: **Řekl, aby tam šla.**

Now, what about "She said we shouldn't arrive late." What is meant here is that some female told a group of people, including the person who is now speaking, that they shouldn't arrive late – i.e. "She said <u>that</u> we shouldn't arrive late". The conditional mood of the first person plural is **bychom** which means that you will use **<u>a</u>bychom.** This will, of course, be the second word in the sentence, so we have **Řekla, abychom nepřišli pozdě.**

Now you have a go.

Exercise 17.5

Complete the following sentences using the conjunction aby and the conditional mood of the verbs in brackets.

1   Řekl ti, ... (vrátit)?

2   Řekli vám, ... (přijet) už v sobotu?

3   Řekla nám, ... tam (zavolat)?

4   Požádal je, ... mu (pomoci).

5   Odjel na hory, ... (odpočinout si).

6   Připomněl nám to několikrát, ... (nezapomenout).

7   Chtěli, ... (my – zůstat) tam s nimi.

8   Chcete, ... (já – přinést) ten nákup?

9   Její manžel nechce, ... (ona – pracovat).

10 Chtěli bychom, ... (vy – cítit se) tady dobře.

17.13 Other uses of *aby*

Aby can be used when English would use a phrase such as "so that", "in order to" or "so's" – in other words, when you're explaining your reason for doing something. Look at the following examples; **aby** covers all of the underlined English constructions.

Šel jsem na hrad, abych viděl jak je krásný.
I went to the castle in order to see how beautiful it is.

Četl jsem tu stránku mluvnice, abych se jí naučil.
I read that page of grammar so that I would learn it.

Podíval jsem se na to znovu, abych si to dobře zapamatoval.
I looked at it again so I'd remember it well.

Vocabulary

architektura (f)	architecture
baroko (n)	baroque
barvoslepý	colour-blind (**barva** (f) – colour; **slepý** – blind)
bydlet; bydlit	to live
časopis (m)	magazine; journal
dovolená (f)	holiday
džezový (adj)	jazz
expedice (f)	expedition
gramofonová deska (f)	gramophone record
hluk (m)	noise
choulostivý	sensitive
jaro (n)	spring (season)
klub (m)	club
květ (m)	flower; blossom
lákat	to attract; call
lidový (adj)	folk
loďka (f)	small (rowing) boat
"Má Vlast" (f)	literally: "My Country", a symphonic poem by Smetana
místo (n)	place
mluvnice (f)	grammar
nákup (m)	shopping
názor (m)	opinion
nejen . . . ale	not only . . . but (also)
několikrát	several times
některý	some
než	than; before
obvykle	usually
odpočinout si	to have a rest; relax

ochutnat	to taste
pára (*f*)	steam
parník (*m*)	steam-boat
pěší zóna (*f*)	pedestrian zone
požádat	to ask; demand
pozdě	ate
pravda (*f*)	truth
Pražské Jaro	Prague Spring (arts festival in Prague)
proslulý	famous
provoz (*m*)	traffic
před	before; in front of
překrásné	"pře-" conveys the idea of "surpassingly"
příběh (*m*)	story; event
připomenout	to remind; recall
půjčit	to lend; loan
půjčit si	to borrow
radši (*adv*)	rather
rockový (*adj*)	rock
Rudolfinum	concert hall in Prague
Secese (*f*)	Art Nouveau (Secession)
senná rýma (*f*)	hayfever (from **seno** (*n*) hay; **ryma** (*f*) cold)
stránka (*f*)	page
symfonická báseň (*f*)	symphonic poem
telefonní seznam (*m*)	telephone directory
trpět	to suffer
turista (*m*)	tourist
ukázat	to show; point; indicate
uslyšet	to hear (perfective)
uvidět	to see (perfective)
ven (*adv*)	out; outward
začít	to begin
záležet	to matter; count
zase (*adv*)	again
zde	here
zrovna	just
ztrácet	to waste

17.14 Dialogue

DIALOGUE

A: Teď budu čtrnáct dní v Praze. Poradil byste mi kam
bych měl jít?

B: V Praze je tolik k vidění! Je to určitě nejkrásnější město
na světě. Ta architektura! Baroko, Secese . . . .

A: Ale v ulicích je velký provoz. A pěší zóna je plná turistů.

B: Tak si půjčte loďku, nebo jeďte na výlet parníkem.

A: Ale já se bojím vody.

B: Aha. Chtěl byste teda jít do parku? Teď na jaře jsou
pražské parky a zahrady opravdu krásné. Nezapomeňte
se jít také podívat do zahrad Hradu, všechno tam kvete
– je květen . . . .

A: Bohužel trpím sennou rýmou.

B: A co divadlo? Ve Stavovském divadle dávají Dona
Giovanniho od Mozarta, a v Národnim divadle dávají
opery od Antonína Dvořáka a Bedřicha Smetany. Znáte
některé?

A: Doma máme gramofonové desky "Má Vlast". To je,
myslím, od Smetany.

B: Ale to není opera, to je symfonická báseň! Možná, že
byste radši šel na koncert.

A: Hmm, možná.

B: Máte štestí. Příští týden začíná hudebni festival
"Pražské Jaro". Jděte na koncert do Rudolfína, kde
nejen uslyšíte krásnou hudbu, ale i uvidíte překrásné
interiéry.

A: Abych vám pravdu řekl, já klasickou hudbu nemám
rád.

B: To nevadí. V Praze jsou džezové kluby, rockové
koncerty, lidová hudba . . . .

A: Hmm . . . jsem trochu choulostivý na hluk.

B: A co nějaké výstavy?

A: Jsem barvoslepý.

B: Tak nevím. Řekněte mi sám, so vás láká.

A: Zrovna teď mám žízeň.

B: No, prosím. Čechy jsou proslulé svým pivem. A v Praze je tolik hospod a pivovarů – na to, abyste ochutnal všechny druhy piva budete potřebovat víc než dva týdny.

A: To je ale dobrý nápad! Děkuju vám. Neměl bych tedy ztrácet čas. Myslím, že začnu hned. Mohu vás pozvat na pivo?

B: Bohužel nemám čas. Jdu zrovna na koncert.

TRANSLATION

A: I am going to be in Prague for two weeks. Would you advise me on where I should go?

B: There is so much to see in Prague! It surely is the most beautiful city in the world. The architecture! Baroque, Art Nouveau . . . .

A: But there's lots of traffic in the streets. And the pedestrian zone is full of tourists.

B: So hire a small boat, or go for a trip in a steam-boat.

A: But I'm afraid of water.

B: I see. So would you like to go to a park? Now, in Spring, Prague's parks and gardens are truly beautiful. Don't forget to see the Castle gardens as well, everything there is in blossom – it's May . . . .

A: Unfortunately, I suffer from hayfever.

B: And what (about) the theatre? At the Stavovské Theatre there's Don Giovanni by Mozart, and at the National Theatre they're doing operas by Antonín Dvořák and Bedřich Smetana. Do you know any (of them)?

A: At home we've got gramophone records of "Má Vlast". I think that's by Smetana.

B: But that's not an opera, that's a symphonic poem! Maybe you'd rather go to a concert.

A: Well, maybe.

B: You're in luck. Next week the music festival "Pražské Jaro" begins. Go to a concert at the Rudolfínum, where you'll not only hear beautiful music, but also see overwhelmingly beautiful interiors.

A: To tell you the truth, I don't like classical music.

B: Doesn't matter. In Prague, there are jazz clubs, rock concerts, folk music . . . .

A: Hmm . . . I am a little sensitive to noise.

B: And what about some exhibitions?

A: I'm colour-blind.

B: Well, I don't know. Tell me yourself: what appeals to you?

A: Right now I'm thirsty.

B: There we are then (literally: well, please). Bohemia is famous for its beer. There are so many pubs and breweries in Prague – (in order) to taste all the varieties of beer, you'd need more than the fortnight.

A: What a good idea! Thank you. I shouldn't waste any time, then, don't you think? I think I'll start right now. Can I invite you for a beer?

B: Sorry, haven't got time. I'm (just) on my way to a concert.

Chapter 18

- *Nouns, adjective and pronouns in the instrumental plural*
- *Negation in a Czech sentence*
- *Diminutives*
- *Final word*

18.1 Nouns: instrumental plural

So, here's the final table of nouns. The instrumental plural is compared with the singular.

	Hard		Soft	
Gender	Singular	Plural	Singular	Plural
Masculine animate	studentem	studenty	mužem	muži
Masculine inanimate	mostem	mosty	pokojem	pokoji
Feminine ("a" or "e" ending)	ženou	ženami	židlí	židlemi
(consonant ending)	místností	místnostmi	skříní	skříněmi
Neuter	městem	městy	mořem	moři
("e" or "i" ending)	náměstím	náměstími	děvčetem	děvčaty

18.2 Adjectives: instrumental plural

This is possibly the easiest ever:

(a) hard adjectives add **-mi** to the nominative singular form, thus: nový**mi**
(b) soft adjectives also add **-mi** to the nominative singular form, thus: modphoní**mi**.

This applies to all genders.

18.3 Demonstrative pronouns: instrumental plural

Gender	Singular	Plural
Masculine	s tím	**s těmi**
Feminine	s tou	**s těmi**
Neuter	s tím	**s těmi**

18.4 Possessive pronouns: instrumental plural

	Masculine		Feminine		Neuter	
	Singular	Plural	Singular	Plural	Singular	Plural
my	mým	mými	mou	mými	mým	mými
your	tvým	tvými	tvou	tvými	tvým	tvými
his and its	jeho	jeho	jeho	jeho	jeho	jeho
her	její	jejími	její	jejími	její	jejími
our	naším	našimi	naší	našimi	naším	našimi
your	vaším	vašimi	vaší	vašimi	vaším	vašimi
their	jejich	jejich	jejich	jejich	jejich	jejich
reflexive	svým	svými	svou	svými	svým	svými

Now apply the information in the tables to the following exercise.

Exercise 18.1

Complete the following sentences by putting the expressions in the brackets into the instrumental plural.

1 Už jsem mluvil s (pracovník) .... vaší firmy.

2 Co jsi udělal s (ta věc) ....?

3 Byli (dobrý student) .... a stali se také (dobrý lékař) ....

4 Po Praze jsme jezdili (tramvaj) .... a samozřejmě také metrem.

5 Setkali jsem se tam se (zajímavý muž) .... s (cizinec) .... i s (Čech) ....

6 Venku bylo teplo a (otevřené okno) .... proudil do místnosti čerstvý vzduch.

7 Nepřipravila to sama, ale se (její kamarádka) ....

8 Ještě jsme se nerozloučili s (dívka) .... z naší třídy.

9 (Praha) .... jsme projeli rychle, ale bylo hezké projíždět (tichá noční ulice) ....

10 Ještě jsme se nedomluvili s (náš soused) ....

18.5 Negation in a Czech sentence

This is one aspect of Czech which you needn't spend too much time learning from the book. It is an idiomatic feature – an important characteristic of the language as used by native speakers – which you'll absorb naturally after substantial exposure to the spoken language.

The sentence "I never done nothing" is incorrect English because it contains a double negative ("never" and "nothing"), one cancelling out the other so that in effect it means "I did something" – quite the opposite of the speaker's intention.

In Czech, however, this doubling of the negation is quite acceptable; it serves to <u>reinforce</u> the negative sense of the sentence and not to dilute or cancel it. Nor are we restricted to doubling – you can have as many negatives in the sentence as you wish. Have a look at **Nikoho jsem nikde neviděl**: translated literally, word for word, this produces "I didn't see nobody nowhere" (three negatives). It <u>means</u> "I didn't see anybody anywhere" (one negative).

The following table shows some of the interrogative pronouns, together with possible answers in generalized terms. It is these pronouns which are most commonly used, along with the **ne-** prefix negating the verb, to form such constructions.

Interrogative		Positive		Negative	
kdo?	who?	**někdo**	(somebody)	**nikdo**	(nobody)
co?	what?	**něco**	(something)	**nic**	(nothing)
kde?	where?	**někde**	(somewhere)	**nikde**	(nowhere)
kam?	where to?	**někam**	(anywhere)	**nikam**	(nowhere)
kdy?	when?	**někdy**	(sometimes)	**nikdy**	(never)
kolik?	how many	**některý**	(some)	**žádný**	(none)

Now look at this sentence: **Nikdo nikdy nemluvil o ničem takovém** (four negatives). With the help of the table above, you can see that a literal translation is: "Nobody never talked about nothing like that". As you will see, these pronouns must be declined – "about nothing" requires the locative case – and they follow the pattern of the demonstrative pronouns (**ten, ta, to**). The English rendering of this would be: "Nobody ever talked about anything like that" (one negative).

Exercise 18.2

You have a go now, by answering the following questions in the negative. Begin with **"Ne, ..."**.

1   Někdo přišel?

2   Byl jsi někdy v Londýně?

3   Některý z nich to včera koupil?

4   Máš nějakou takovou knihu?

5   Mluvil jsi s někým?

6   Poslal jsi někomu pohled?

7   Viděli jste někde někoho známého?

8   O něčem takovém neslyšela?

9   Řekneš mi to někdy?

18.6 Diminutives

Diminutives can be used to indicate that something is small (as in the English "piglet" as compared to "pig", "booklet" as compared to "book", for example) or to demonstrate an affection for something or someone. As the above examples show, a diminutive isn't necessarily a shorter word than that to which it relates. One of the most common uses of diminutive forms in English is in relation to Christian names: Anne and Annie; Daniel and Danny; Thomas and Tommy. The "-ie" or "-y" suffix is not the only way to make a diminutive, but it is probably the most usual one. Czech also has ways of shortening names and, as in English, the use of a diminutive, as well as indicating smallness of size, can indicate familiarity, close friendship, affection – and, as we shall see, a great deal more.

We shall look first at some standard diminutive forms, and then we'll show you how Czech can be extremely expressive and creative – especially with diminutives of Christian names.

18.7 Standard uses of diminutives

Diminutive endings for <u>masculine</u> nouns include: **-ek, -ík, -eček, -íček, -ínek**. Let's take **táta** (dad) as a first example. In English, this is itself a diminutive – but the further English diminutive, "daddy" usually connotes a softer degree of affection, or the greater dependence of the younger child. **Tatínek** would be the equivalent expression in Czech – but the teenage daughter wanting permission to stay out late might go for **tatíníček**. Uncle Joe is **strýc Pepík** – but a "special" Uncle Joe could be **strýček Pepíček**.

Of course, diminutives are also used just to convey the idea of smallness, so the diminutive endings listed above can be used with any masculine noun. A "little tree", for example, could be **stromek** or **stromeček**.

As you might expect, the <u>feminine</u> diminutive endings end in **-a**, so **Anna** could become An**ka** to her family, and she might call her mother **mamička**. One you ought to watch out for here: **babička** is the word for a grandmother or a <u>nice</u> old woman, and **babka** is a <u>little</u> old woman, but **bába** is <u>NOT</u> a more formal way in which to address an elderly woman – it contains an element of "hag". Don't use it unless you <u>want</u> to be rude! If you <u>do</u> want to be rude (which we don't advise) then you can turn the heat up with **babice** (horrible hag) and **babizna** (the same, but more so!). Interestingly, you can't do the same with "<u>grandfather</u>": from **dědeček** (grandfather), you can have **děda** (a little old man), **dědula** (a sweet little old man) and **dědek** which, depending on context, can be affectionate or not. An <u>affectionate</u> insult could be **dědour**.

<u>Neuter</u> nouns can take diminutives such as **-ko, -ečko, -ičko, -íčko**, thus a small town (**město**) of which you were fond, or which tourist literature might describe as "quaint" could become "**městečko**".

18.8 Diminutives which change the meaning of the original noun

Sometimes the meaning of a diminutive can be significantly different from the original noun. Here are some examples.

hodiny (*f*)	hours; clock	**hodinky** (*pl*)	watch
chléb (*m*)	bread	**chlebíček** (*m*)	open sandwich
škola (f)	school	**školka** (f)	nursery; kindergarten

18.9 Diminutives of adjectives and adverbs

There are diminutive forms of adjectives and adverbs as well as of nouns, such as:

malý	ma**link**ý
málo	ma**link**o
hezký	hez**ouč**ký
pomalu	pomal**ouč**ku

Note, though, that it is not necessary to use a diminutive form of adjective with a diminutive form of the noun. Although a diminutive adjective would strengthen the effect of using a diminutive noun, in almost every case, to add the diminutive to the noun alone will be sufficient.

18.10 Creative use of diminutives

What we are talking about here are the sorts of additions to Christian names which English people tend to use only in private – or perhaps in Valentine Day messages in newspapers. A girl called Anne could be called Annie by her family and friends in virtually any situation without anyone being caused any embarrassment. In private, however, her boyfriend might call her Annikins – less shout-able in the supermarket, to say the least.

But look at this range of possible diminutive endings for a Czech girl called Anna: Anka, Anička, Andulka, Anuška, Anča, Ančička, Andulinka. These are all what we would call "pet" names. They're fairly interchangeable but, generally speaking, the longer the diminutive ending, the more passionate the affection behind it! Be inventive with these should you ever find yourself in a situation where you feel it befitting to use them: you can make them up, string them together and – if the situation really is appropriate – grammar takes second place to emotion!

The final dialogue of the course demonstrates this creativity (as it's impossible to give literal translations of the degrees of endearment implied by the different forms, we've used English expressions which should be regarded as "rough emotional equivalents"!!).

Vocabulary

domluvit se	to agree; come to an agreement; make oneself understood
noční (*adj*)	night
pracovník (*m*)	worker
proč	why? what . . . for?
proudit	to flow; to stream
rozloučit se	to say goodbye; take leave
sama	alone (when applied to the feminine; *m* = **sám;** *n* = **samo)**
sbohem	farewell; goodbye
vzduch (*m*)	air

18.11 Dialogue

DIALOGUE

Petr: Dobrý večer, Aničko.

Anna: Dobrý večer, Petře.

Petr: Tak rád tě vidím, Aninko.

Anna: Péťo . . .

Petr: Jak se máš, Andulko?

Anna: Mám se moc dobře, děkuju, Peťulko.

Petr: Ančičko, kdy budeš má?

Anna: Ale, Petříku, vždyť víš, že nemohu.

Petr: Proč? Anuško, Anduličko?

Anna: Ty víš proč.

Petr: Co je na tom, mé kuřátko, má holubičko, má růžičko, můj pavoučíčku . . . .

Anna: Prestaň.

Petr: Anko, Ančičko, Andulinko, Andulčicko, nemohu dál čekat!

Anna: Petříku, není to možné. Můj muž . . . .

Petr: Anno!

Anna: Sbohem, pane Liško.

TRANSLATION

Peter: Good evening, Anna dear.

Anna: Good evening, Peter.

Peter: I am so glad to see you, dear Annie.

Anna: Peter dear . . .

Peter: How are you, Annie dearest?

Anna: I'm very well, thank you, Peter dear.

Peter: Beloved Annie, when will you be mine?

Anna: But Peter, darling, you know I can't.

Peter: Why, dearest, dearest Annie?

Anna: You know why.

Peter: What does it matter, my little chicken, my little dove, my little rose, my tiny spider?

Anna: Stop this.

Peter: Annie, my beloved, Annie, my sweet, Annie, my life, I can't wait any more!

Anna: It's impossible, Peter dear. My husband . . . .

Peter: Anna!

Anna: Adieu, Mr Liška.

Final word: Where am I, dictionaries, and where do I go from here?

Where am I?
In the Introduction, we offered to provide a mid-point between the phrase-book, with its fixed-function sound-bites on the one hand, and a highly detailed and comprehensive coverage of Czech grammar on the other. In answer to the question, "Where am I?", then, we would hope that, having completed the course, you now have a clear understanding of the basic grammar we have taught and that, with the help of a dictionary, you will be able to construct most of the concepts you might wish to express.

Dictionaries
A word about dictionaries. As yet (spring 1995), there is no Czech–English/English–Czech dictionary of the calibre of the Collins or Oxford foreign language dictionaries. Of those which are available, we would recommend the *Hippocrene Concise Dictionary* by Nina Trnka (revised edition, 1991) largely because it gives the genders of the nouns. However, should one of the well-established British dictionary publishers have produced a Czech–English/English–Czech dictionary by the time you come to be considering your purchase, then we would recommend that you buy one of those in preference.

The words in the vocabulary lists in the chapters have been set out in the order in which they would appear in a Czech dictionary, and you should note the following points.
(a) words beginning with **ch** come after those beginning with the letter **h**
(b) words beginning with **č** are listed in a separate alphabetical list after those beginning with **c**, and the same applies to **ř** and **r**, **š** and **s**, and **ž** and **z**
(c) the same rules apply when these letters appear in the middles of words – when a háček is involved, the letter <u>with</u> the háček will come <u>after</u> the letter without it: thus, to take **r** and **ř** as examples, we would have, in dictionary order, **struna**, **strýc**, **středa**, etc.
(d) these are the only instances in which accent affects dictionary word-order.

Where do I go from here?

The answer depends very much on <u>how</u> you want to expand your facility in Czech, and on where you live. If you are a business person, your company may sponsor further courses of study at a private language college for you to develop specific vocabulary and formal etiquette for negotiations in your company's field of business; if you used this course as a "toe in the water" for academic study of a subject in which there is a substantial amount of literature in Czech, you may find that the languages department of your local university may be able to help; if you intend to study the Czech language or literature itself, then you have a fair way to go but, again, your local university or the School of Slavonic and Eastern European Studies of the University of London should be able to advise; if you have studied for the purposes of a visit to the Czech Republic, then perhaps you have been in contact with a Czech speaker, or can make contact with a Czech speaker, who will help you to acquire the colloquial fluency you would wish to have in social situations.

Whatever your further ambitions, we hope you have enjoyed working through this course and wish you every success.

Key to Exercises

Exercise 1.1: obviously, the answers cannot be written down! You should refer to the cassette which accompanies the course for confirmation that your pronunciation is correct.

Exercise 2.1: Masculine: prezident; parlament; bratr; Petr. **Feminine:** matka; žízeň; sestra; Martina; restaurace. **Neuter:** auto; divadlo; kino; moře.

Exercise 2.2: (a): (i) jste. (ii) jsi. (iii) je. (iv) jsem. (v) jsou. (vi) jsme. **(b):** (i) nejsem. (ii) není. (iii) nejste. (iv) nejsme. (v) nejsi. (vi) není. (vii) nejsou. **(c):** (i) my. (ii) oni (ony, ona). (iii) ty. (iv) já. (v) on (ona, ono). (vi) on (ona, ono). (vii) vy.

Exercise 2.3: 1 Má. 2 Mají. 3 Máš. 4 Máte. 5 Má. 6 Má OR mají. 7 Nemám. 8 Mají. 9 Máš. 10 Nemáme.

Exercise 2.4: (a): B: Dobrý den. A: máte. B: dobře. B: Na shledanou. **(b):** A: Ahoj. A: se máš. B: Děkuji. A: děkuji. B: Ahoj. A: Ahoj.

Exercise 2.5: 1 Náš nový dům. 2 Jeho velká kniha. 3 Jejich moderní byt. 4 Mé čisté okno. 5 Tvá bílá káva. 6 Její krásný stůl. 7 Jejich cizí auto.

Exercise 2.6:

(a) Kdo je to?   To je dítě.
    Jaké je to dítě?   To je malé dítě. (OR To dítě je malé.)
    Je to dítě hodné?   Ano, je./Ne, není.

(b) Kdo je to?   To je dívka.
    Jaká je ta dívka?   To je vysoká dívka. (OR Ta dívka je vysoká.)
  Je ta dívka mladá?   Ano, je./Ne, není.

(c)	Kdo je to?	To je doktor.
	Jaký je ten doktor?	To je český doktor. (OR Ten doktor je Čech.)
	Je ten doktor dobrý?	Ano, je./Ne, není.
(d)	Co je to?	To je okno.
	Jaká je to okno?	To je velké okno. (OR To okno je velké.)
	Je to okno čisté?	Ano, je./Ne, není.
(e)	Co je to?	To je židle.
	Jaká je ta židle?	To je stará židle. (OR Ta židle je stará.)
	Je ta židle hezká?	Ano, je./Ne, není.
(f)	Co je to?	To je park.
	Jaký je ten park?	To je velký park. (OR Ten park je velký.)
	Je ten park krásný?	Ano, je./Ne, není.

Exercise 2.7: 1 Either they don't know each other well, or their relationship is a formal one: **dobrý den** (good morning) is a formal greeting as it is in English; they use the formal form of "you" **(vy)**. 2 In the case of the woman, **studentka** is used, which denotes a female student, and the adjective endings are feminine (**mladá; nová**); in the case of the man **mladý** is the male form of the adjective.

Exercise 3.1: 1 Paní Nováková má učebnici. 2 Ten Angličan má přítelkyni. 3 Máme byt. 4 Ta dáma má růži. 5 Nemá židli.

Exercise 3.2: 1 Paní Nováková má novou učebnici. 2 Ten Angličan má mladou přítelkyni. 3 Máme čistý byt. 4 Ta dáma má krásnou růži. 5 Nemá velkou židli.

Exercise 3.3: 1 Má je? 2 Máte ji? 3 Máme ho/její? 4 Má ho/jej/je? 5 Má ho/jej? 6 Má ho/jej/je?

Exercise 3.4: 1 Mám její knihu. 2 Má jejich pokoj. 3 Máte naše kolo. 4 Má nové pero. 5 Máš/Máte mou (moji) knihu? 6 Mají nový byt. Jejich nový byt není čistý. 7 Můj bratr má můj stůl; já mám jeho židli. 8 Jeho dívka má hezkou růži. 9 Nemá mou (moji) tašku? 10 Naše město má velké náměstí.

Exercise 4.1: prodávám, prodáváš, prodává, prodáváme, prodáváte, prodávají.

Exercise 4.2: 1 Hledáme dům. 2 Prodávám auto. 3 Dívá se na moře. 4 Hledají úředníka. 5 Ta dívka odpovídá na otázku. 6 Díváte se na toho muže. Snídá. 7 Obědváš. Je to kuře? 8 Učitel poslouchá tu dívku.

Exercise 4.3: 1 děláte. 2 nedělají. 3 nedělám. 4 děláš. 5 dělá. 6 neděláme.

Exercise 4.4: 1 Nehledají tašku. 2 Neprodávám kolo. 3 Neotvírá dveře. 4 Neděláme tu věc. 5 Neprodává knihy. 6 Nehledáte nádraží. 7 Netrháš ovoce.

Exercise 4.5: 1 Pan Novák je ženatý. 2 Paní Nováková je vdaná. 3 Pan Novák a paní Novaková jsou rodiče. 4 Rodina je otec, matka, bratr a sestra. 5 Bratr je rozvedený; jmenuje se Karel. 6 Sestra je vdaná; jmenuje se Jana. 7 Bratr neposlouchá rodiče. 8 Stará teta je svobodná. Paní Nováková je její sestra.

Exercise 5.1: 1 studujeme. 2 studuje? 3 studují (OR studujou). 4 (ne)studuješ. 5 pracujete. 6 pracuje; pracujeme. 7 potřebujete. 8 (ne)potřebuji (OR (ne)potřebuju), potřebuje. 9 miluji (OR miluju). 10 miluje. 11 ohrožují (OR ohrožujou). 12 ohrožuje. 13 kupuješ. 14 kupuji (OR kupuju). 15 kupuje. 16 telefonuje. 17 telefonují (OR telefonujou). 18 netelefonuješ.

Exercise 5.2: 1 Potřebuji (OR potřebuju) jídlo. 2 Ten muž kupuje auto. 3 Pěstujeme krásnou novou růži. 4 Kupují velkou skříň. 5 Miluji (OR miluju) její dceru. 6 Nepotřebujete (OR nepotřebujete) tu knihu, ale kupuješ (OR kupujete) ji. 7 Opakujeme tu píseň. 8 Studujete gramatiku? 9 Ty nemiluješ slečnu Novákovou? 10 Hodně (*or* moc) děkují (OR Hodně (*or* moc) děkujou).

Exercise 5.3: 1 obraz Prahy (a picture of Prague). 2 okno pokoje (a window of a room). 3 budova pošty (a building of a post-office). 4 ovoce ostrova (fruit of the island). 5 číslo autobusu (a number of a bus). 6 kniha studenta (a student's book). 7 plán města (a plan of a city). 8 fotografie přítelkyně (a photograph of a girlfriend). 9 auto přitele (a boyfriend's car). 10 láhev vína (a bottle of wine).

Exercise 5.4: 1 kousek sýra (a small piece of cheese). 2 sklenice vína (a glass of wine). 3 láhev piva (a bottle of beer). 4 kousek másla (a little bit of butter). 5 kus chleba (a chunk of bread). 6 trochu cukru (a little sugar). 7 hodně vody (a lot of water). 8 mnoho práce (a lot of work). 9 málo času (a little time). 10 šálek kávy (a cup of coffee).

Exercise 5.5: *Any of* mnoho/málo/hodně/trochu *in front of* : 1 indického čaje. 2 černé kávy. 3 dobrého masa. 4 čerstvé zeleniny. 5 pražské šunky. 6 cizí zeleniny. 7 zahraničního ovoce.

Exercise 5.6: 1 Pracujeme od rána do večera. 2 To je mapa Prahy. 3 Potřebuji tolik cukru. 4 Mám jen trochu polévky. 5 To je pěkný obraz pražského hradu. 6 Tady je jenom trochu soli.

Exercise 5.7: 1 bez nich. 2 kvůli mě. 3 kromě mě (OR mne). 4 ho/jej. 5 jich, jí. 6 jeho.

Exercise 5.8: 1 jeho (*in this sentence, for emphasis*) nebo jí. 2 vedle ní. 3 jí. 4 Jistě si ho nevšimne. 5 ho. 6 vedle nich.

Exercise 5.9: 1 Jméno mého bratra. 2 Auto mé sestry. 3 Barva tvé židle. 4 Dveře našeho domu. 5 Je to tvá kniha? Ne, to je kniha mého bratra.

Exercise 5.10: A: I am afraid of that person. B: This one? A: No. That one. B: I see! This one.

Exercise 5.11: 1 mého manžela. 2 tvého přítele. 3 toho domu. 4 toho nového studenta a té nové studentky. 5 Nový obchodní dům je vedle vašeho domu. 6 To je knížka té hezké dívky. 7 Všichni jsou tam, vyjma našeho přítele. 8 To je adresa naší firmy.

Exercise 6.1: A: mluví. B: nemluví. A: mluvíte. B: mluvíme; mluvím. A: mluví.

Exercise 6.2: 1 Zdraví tu Američanku. 2 Kde to vidíš? 3 Jana prosí o ovoce. 4 Sedí tamhle. 5 Vždycky nosíš těžkou tašku. 6 Myslím, že je krásná. 7 Myslí, že to je lehký test. 8 Co slyšíš. 9 Kde leží ta kniha? 10 Teď učí angličtinu v Praze.

Exercise 6.3: 1 přicházejí; přichází; přicházím. 2 víte; nevíme; ví. 3 rozumí; nerozumějí; rozumíš; nerozumím. 4 jedí; nejíme. 5 vím. 6 rozumíš.

Exercise 6.4: 1 rozumím; nerozumí. 2 studují; nestudujeme. 3 pracuje, nepracují. 4 mluvím; nemluví. 5 jedí; nejí. 6 dělám/děláme; neděláš. 7 vím/víme; nevědí. 8 přicházejí; nepřicházím. 9 jím; nejíte. 10 končím; nekončí.

Exercise 7.1: 1 Co čtete? 2 Nečtu to. 3 Kdo to čte? 4 Nečtou tu knihu. 5 Často čteme. 6 Ty nečteš?

Exercise 7.2: 1 Jede tam. 2 Jdou. 3 Jdu. 4 Jde. 5 Nejedeme tam. 6 Nejdeš. 7 Jdou nebo jedou? 8 Nejde; jede. 9 Jedete. 10 Nejede.

Exercise 8.1: 1 V Praze jsou divadla, kina, mosty, ulice, obchody, náměstí, kostely, paláce. 2 V Praze žijí muži, ženy, dívky, studenti, cizinci, kočky. 3 Jsou vánoce. V obchodě jsou láhve vína, lahůdky, krůty, krocani, husy. 4 Tady prodávají nábytek. Tady jsou skříně, židle, postele, stoly, křesla a také obrazy.

Exercise 8.2: 1 V Praze žijí Češi, kluci, doktoři, úředníci. 2 Jsou velikonoce. V obchodě jsou kapři a pstruzi. 3 Vy neznáte ty chlapce? To jsou bratři. 4 Kdo hraje fotbal? Kluci hrají.

Exercise 8.3: 1 strozí. 2 tiší. 3 velcí. 4 dobří.

Exercise 8.4: 1 Tady jsou čeští studenti. 2 To jsou sympatičtí přátelé. 3 To jsou velcí kapři. 4 Přijedou angličtí sportovci. 5 To jsou strozí učitelé.

Exercise 8.5: 1 To jsou staré stoly. 2 To jsou čeští studenti. 3 Ty obchodní domy jsou velké. 4 Ta okna jsou velká. 5 To jsou sympatičtí chlapci. 6 Tam jsou teplá moře. 7 To jsou velcí a čerství pstruzi. 8 To už nejsou malí hoši, to jsou velcí hoši. 9 To jsou dobří doktoři. 10 To jsou zajímavé knihy.

Exercise 8.6: 1 Vidíme české studenty. 2 Máme sympatické přátele. 3 Mají velké kapry. 4 Uvidíme anglické sportovce. 5 Máme strohé učitele.

Exercise 9.1: 1 Studovali jsme. 2 Viděl jsme ten film. 3 Dělali polévku. 4 Kupovali jste svetr. 5 Mluvila včera. 6 Chtěl jsi knihu.

Exercise 9.2: 1 neměli. 2 jsem nejedl OR nejedla. 3 jsem nešel OR nešla. 4 nebyl. 5 jsem nestudoval. 6 kupoval. 7 jsem ...... měl. 8 se vrátil. 9 jsi ...... pil. 10 jsem šel OR šla.

Exercise 9.3: Včera ráno jsem vstal. Byl hezký den. Chtěl jsem jít do města. Odpoledne jsem šel do restaurace. Měl jsem kávu (dal jsem si kávu). Začal jsem číst novou knihu. Potom jsem potkal přítele a nečetl jsem. Můj přítel jedl zeleninový salát. Neměl jsem hlad, ale měl jsem žízeň. Pil jsem šťávu.

Exercise 9.4: 1 Máte tady nějaké české knihy? (Do you have any Czech books here?) 2 Viděli jsme tam naše známé. (We saw our acquaintances there.) 3 Koupili čokoládové bonbóny. (They bought chocolates (chocolate sweets).) 4 Tamhle vidím nějaké autobusy, ale ne číslo 11. (I can see some buses over there, but not the number 11.) 5 Máme české knihy. (We have Czech books.) 6 Koupili anglická auta. (They have bought English cars.) 7 Mají hezké fotografie. (They have nice photographs.) 8 Viděli velká a malá města. (They saw large and small towns.)

Exercise 9.5: 1 dobrých knih. 2 židlí. 3 českých slov. 4 korun; haléřů. 5 našich rodičů. 6 studentů. 7 galerií, zajímavých obrazů. 8 zkoušek. 9 starostí. 10 těch chlapců a dívek.

Exercise 9.6: 1 Kolik je tam pokojů? Jsou tam čtyři malé pokoje, ale mnoho velkých pokojů. 2 Kolik velkých skříní je tam? Jsou tam jenom tři velké skříně. 3 Kolik moderních aut jste tam viděli? Viděli jsme tam čtyři moderní auta, ale jedno velmi staré auto. 4 Kolik mužů a žen se zúčastnilo toho maratónu? Čtyři ženy, mnoho mužů. 5 Kolik historických domů stojí na náměstí? 6 Kolik velkých stolů máte doma? Máme dva velké stoly. 7 Kolik českých studentů tady máte? Máme tady čtyři. Ti čeští studenti právě přicházejí. 8 Kolik dívek se zúčastnilo finále MISS? Myslím, že to bylo dvanáct krásných dívek, ale jenom tři vyhrály. 9 Kolik přátel jsi pozval? Pozval jsem všechny, ale jenom čtyři přátellé nepřišli.

Exercise 9.7: 1 čtvrtého listopadu. 2 třicátého září. 3 dvacátého čtvrtého června. 4 sedmnáctého srpna. 5 šestého listopadu. 6 pátého prosince. 7 třetího ledna. 8 třináctého února. 9 druhého března. 10 třicátého dubna. 11 pátého května. 12 čtvrtého července. 13 sedmého října.

Exercise 10.1: 1 Rád (OR Ráda, *depending on whether you are male or female*) piju (OR piji) kávu. 2 Ráda jí knedlíky. 3 Neradi jsme tady. 4 *Informal:* Máš rád (OR ráda) knihy. *Formal:* Máte rád (OR ráda) knihy. 5 Mají rádi Prahu? 6 Nemám rád (OR ráda, *depending on whether you are male or female*) pivo. 7 Nerad jí toto jídlo.

Exercise 10.2: 1 Znám jeho manželku. 2 Bohužel nevím, kdo to psal. 3 Víte prosím, kde je tady Dlouhá Ulice? 4 Známe jejich adresu, víme, kde bydlí. 5 Už včera věděl, kdy se vrátíte. 6 Znáš jeho auto? Vím jen, že je červené.

Exercise 10.3: 1 Chci jít do kina, ale nemůžu (OR nemohu). Musím studovat. 2 Je to možné koupit tady cukr? Může se tady koupit cukr? 3 Nesmíš to říkat. 4 Umí česky. 5 Dcera potřebuje svetr. Musím ho koupit. 6 Můžeme se vrátit ted'. 7 Ivano, chceš jít do divadla? 8 Můžu (OR mohu) otevřít okno? 9 Nemusí to dělat. 10 Musíš zavolat policii.

Exercise 11.1:

	Subject	Direct Object	Indirect Object
1	Mary	a meal	John
2	they	a present	their teacher
3	that letter	– – – – – –	me
4	We	a Merry Christmas	you
5	The council	a grant	the student

6 you (nom.); your prize (acc.); charity (dat.). 7 He (nom.); his daughter's (gen.); book (acc.); children (dat.). 8 letter (nom.); us (dat.). 9 curator (nom.); me (dat.); painting (acc.). 10 film (nom.); I (nom.); you (dat.).

Exercise 11.2: 1 dívce. 2 Olze. 3 knize. 4 střeše. 5 dceři. 6 hoře. 7 sestře.

Exercise 11.3: 1 Nerozumím jen tomu poslednímu slovu, on nerozumí té dlouhé větě. 2 Pomáhají té staré ženě, musíš pomáhat sousedovi, je také starý. 3 Věnujeme se angličtině, je to světový jazyk. 4 Patří ten kabát té neznámé dívce nebo Olze? 5 Dávám přednost kávě, ale on čaji. 6 To není dobré. Škodí to zdraví. 7 Kam jdete? Jdeme na návštěvu k naší nemocné kamarádce. 8 Odpověděl jsem tomu muži.

Exercise 11.4: 1 příteli, tuto zajímavou knihu. 2 bratrovi, tuto fotografii. 3 té dívce, hezkou sukni. 4 přítelkyni, květiny. 5 někomu, něco.

Exercise 11.5: 1 čemu. 2 komu. 3 někomu. 4 něčemu. 5 někomu.

Exercise 11.6: 1 nám, nim. 2 ní. 3 vám. 4 tobě. 5 němu, ní.

Exercise 11.7: 1 jí, jemu. 2 jim. 3 mi, ti. 4 tobě. 5 vám.

Exercise 12.1: 1 Já čtu (tu) knihu. Ona jí přečte později. 2 Ona snídá; my se teď napijeme kávy a naobědváme se později. 3 Čeká jí v sobotu; počká na ní na stanici. 4 Paní Nováková vaří snídani; Jana uvaří večeři. 5 (On) pije pivo; uvidí nás později. 6 Píšete dnes (ten) dopis? Ano, ale dokončím ho zítra.

Exercise 12.2: 1 My na vás počkáme ve tři čtvrtě na dvě. OR Počkáme na vás ve tři čtvrtě na dvě. 2 On se naobědvá v jednu hodinu. 3 Vaříš jídlo na půl osmou. 4 (My) počkáme na vlak v jednu hodinu a dvacet minut. 5 Skončím (v) za pět minut devět. 6 Oni zopakují ten film ve čtvrt na devět.

Exercise 13.1: 1 navštěvuji. 2 počkám. 3 vrátíš. 4 jíst. 5 udělám. 6 obědváme; se naobědváme. 7 platím; zaplatit.

Exercise 13.2: (a) obědvám; odpovídám; platím; uklízím; navštěvuji; hraji. (b) se naobědvám; odpovím; zaplatím; uklidím; navštívím; zahraji.

Exercise 13.3: 1 píše; napíše. 2 nesnídám; snídat. 3 nedělají; udělají. 4 koupí; kupuje. 5 číst (na čtení); přečtu.

Exercise 13.4: 1 (On) platí. 2 Budou to číst. (Přečtou to.) 3 (On) odpoví. 4 Vracíme se. 5 Kde budete večeřet? 6 Piji (Piju) kávu. 7 Mám hlad. Sním celý dort. 8 Navštívím jí. 9 Co kupuješ/kupujete? 10 Nemám žízeň. Napiji/Napiju se jen trochu.

Exercise 13.5: 1 hezky; jasno. 2 česky; dobře. 3 špatně. 4 lehce. 5 anglicky? 6 špatně; dobře (or the reverse!).

Exercise 14.1: B: Jděte; nejděte. B: Jed'te; ale nejed'te. *Translation:* A: Excuse me please, where is there a post-office here? B: Go straight along this street, but not right to the end. A: Thank you, but can you tell me how to get to the museum? B: Take (go by) tram number 18, there's a stop near the post-office, but don't take (go by) tram number 9. A: Thanks very much. B: Don't mention it.

Exercise 14.2: A: udělej (or dělej); **nedělej.** A: Hm, přidej; nepřidej. B: Vezmi si; neber si. *Translation:* A: What are you doing here? B: Well, I want to make (prepare) something for dinner but I don't know what. A: Make the recipe Jane said (was talking about), but don't make too much, we're not very hungry. B: Is it good? A: Hm, add pepper, but not any more salt. It isn't healthy. C: Can I have some too? B: Take a bit (some), but not a lot. C: It's delicious!

Exercise 14.3: 1 o studentce. 2 na podlaze. 3 o sestře. 4 ve sprše. 5 na knize.

Exercise 14.4: 1 V Praze, v Brně, v Bratislavě, v Londýně, v Paříži, v Berlíně, v Hamburku, ve Vídni. 2 O Marii, o Petrovi, o té hezké dívce, o tom novém studentovi, o jeho tetě, o mém známém, o jejím příteli. 3 O české kuchyni, o tom velkém problému, o tom těžkém textu, o tom zajímavém televizním programu, o té nečekané zprávě, o jeho chování. 4 V tašce, v tom velkém stole, v kabelce, v knihovně, v druhém pokoji, v ložnici, v nočním stolku. 5 Na zemi, na podlaze, na židli, na skříni, na koberci. 6 Po obědě, po večeři, po snídani, po představení, po přednášce. 7 Při módní přehlídce, při dopoledním vyučování, při hodině angličtiny, při jejich návštěvě. 8 Na obědě, na večeři, na výstavě, na prohlídce. 9 Ve třídě, v jeho bytě, v jejich domě.

Exercise 14.5: 1 něm. 2 nich. 3 něm. 4 tobě. 5 ní, nás.

Exercise 14.6: 1 Narodil(a) jsem se v červnu. 2 Narodil(a) jsem se v prosinci. 3 Narodil(a) jsem se v dubnu. 4 Narodil(a) jsem se v srpnu. 5 Narodil(a) jsem se v listopadu. 6 Narodil(a) jsem se v březnu.

Exercise 14.7: Prague is the capital of the Czech Republic. It is a beautiful city where there are many historic buildings. Prague Castle is probably the first place visitors would head for. Usually they go over Charles Bridge, an old bridge in the centre of town, from which one has a beautiful view of the Hradčany Castle. If you don't know Prague, you must ask the way.

Exercise 15.1: 1 Slečno Nováková. 2 Evo. 3 Jirko. 4 studente. 5 Láďo.

Exercise 15.2: 1 (Ty) nebudeš rozumět. 2 (On) bude dnes pracovat. 3 (Oni) tam nepůjdou. 4 (Já) nebudu spěchat. 5 Děti, vy půjdete. 6 (My) budeme čekat.

Exercise 15.3: 1 navštívíš. 2 bude čekat. 3 bude dělat. 4 se vrátí. 5 budete jíst ...... sním. 6 uvidíme. 7 budeme se dívat. 8 napsat. 9 se oblékneš. 10 koupit.

Exercise 15.4: 1 se vrátí. 2 přečte. 3 večeřet nebudu. 4 budou se rozhodovat. 5 koupíme. 6 uděláme. 7 budu se ho učit.

Exercise 16.1: 1 jeho přítelem. 2 Ivanou a Pepíkem. 3 autem. 4 vlakem. 5 letadlem. 6 tramvají; metrem. 7 perem; tužkou. 8 tímhle pracím prostředkem. 9 parkem. 10 příborem.

Exercise 16.2: 1 nimi. 2 ní. 3 ním. 4 mnou. 5 tebou. 6 vámi. 7 námi. 8 vámi. 9 tebou; nimi.

Exercise 16.3: 1 rychlejší. 2 nejstarší. 3 dražší. 4 starší; mladší. 5 nejdůležitější. 6 hezčí (nejhezčí). 7 nejzajímavější. 8 mladší. 9 nejkrásnější.

Exercise 16.4: 1 nejlepší. 2 horší. 3 rychlejší. 4 nejlepší. 5 nejzajímavější. 6 lehčí. 7 nejhezčí. 8 menší. 9 praktičtější.

Exercise 16.5: 1 přijede; odjede. 2 odnést; přinést. 3 připravil. 4 odjíždí. 5 přijdeš. 6 přílet. 7 přijede.

Exercise 16.6: 1 sešli; došli. 2 vyšli. 3 odešli. 4 vycházela. 5 Došli. 6 vycházejí. 7 Dojíždíš. 8 přijíždí. 9 odjíždí. 10 sejít.

Exercise16.7: The train came out of the station. It travelled straight for a while, then went up a hill, went down it again, and through a tunnel. When it came out of the tunnel, it travelled over a river and under a tall bridge. At last it arrived at a station.

Exercise 17.1: 1 vašich nových přátelích. 2 restauracích; hotelech. 3 ulicích. 4 těch pokojích. 5 všech židlích. 6 vašich problémech. 7 všech místech. 8 velkých náměstích. 9 starých domech. 10 jejich názorech. 11 Vánocích. 12 Velikonocích. 13 Poděbradech. 14 Domažlicích.

Exercise 17.2: 1 rychleji. 2 nejlépe. 3 horší. 4 nejdále. 5 nejdéle. 6 dříve. 7 nejpozději. 8 nejdále.

Exercise 17.3: 1 Já bych to koupil. 2 bychom se zeptali. 3 by to udělali. 4 bychom to dělali. 5 bychom vám ji ukázali.

Exercise 17.4: 1 Pomohl(a) bys mu? OR Nepomohl(a) bys mu? 2 Podal(a) bys mu tu knihu? OR Nepodal(a) bys mu tu knihu? 3 Šli/Šly byste tam, taky? OR Nešli/nešly byste tam, taky? 4 Vrátil(a) bych se dřív? (Not suitable for negative construction.) 5 Přišli/Přišly byste k nám? OR Nepřišli/Nepřišly byste k nám? 6 Půjčil(a) bys mi ten časopis? OR Nepůjčil(a) bys mi ten časopis? 7 Zavřeli/Zavřely by okno? OR Nezavřeli/Nezavřely by okno? 8 Otevřel(a) bys dveře? OR Neotevřel(a) bys dveře?

Exercise 17.5: 1 aby ses vrátil. 2 abyste přijeli. 3 abychom tam zavolali. 4 aby mu pomohli. 5 aby si odpočinul. 6 abychom nezapoměli. 7 abychom tam s nimi zůstali. 8 abych přinesl. 9 aby pracovala. 10 abyste se tady cítili dobře.

Exercise 18.1: 1 pracovníky. 2 tou věcí. 3 dobrými studenty; dobrými lékaři. 4 tramvajemi. 5 zajímavými muži; cizinci; Čechy. 6 otevřenými okny. 7 jejími kamarádkami. 8 děvčaty. 9 Prahou; tichými nočími ulicemi. 10 našimi sousedy.

Exercise 18.2: 1 Nikdo nepřišel. 2 Nebyl jsi nikdy v Londýně. 3 Nikdo z nich to včera nekoupil. 4 Nemáš žádnou takovou knihu. 5 Nemluvil jsi s nikým. 6 Neposlal jsi nikomu pohled. 7 Neviděli jste nikde žádného známého. 8 O ničem takovém neslyšela. 9 Nikdy mi to neřekneš.

Index